THE ULTIMATE TOWER AIR FRYER COOKBOOK FOR BEGINNERS

1000 Days Quick&Easy And Delicious Air Fryer Homemade Recipes Anyone Can Easily Make At Home On a Budget

CATHERINE C. KIMBREL

Copyright© 2022 By Catherine C. Kimbrel Rights Reserved

This book is copyright protected. It is only for personal use. You cannot amend, distribute, sell, use, quote or paraphrase any part of the content within this book, without the consent of the author or publisher.

Under no circumstances will any blame or legal responsibility be held against the publisher, or author, for any damages, reparation, or monetary loss due to the information contained within this book, either directly or indirectly.

Disclaimer Notice:

Please note the information contained within this document is for educational and entertainment purposes only. All effort has been executed to present accurate, up to date, reliable, complete information. No warranties of any kind are declared or implied. Readers acknowledge that the author is not engaged in the rendering of legal, financial, medical or professional advice. The content within this book has been derived from various sources. Please consult a licensed professional before attempting any techniques outlined in this book.

By reading this document, the reader agrees that under no circumstances is the author responsible for any losses, direct or indirect, that are incurred as a result of the use of the information contained within this document, including, but not limited to, errors, omissions, or inaccuracies.

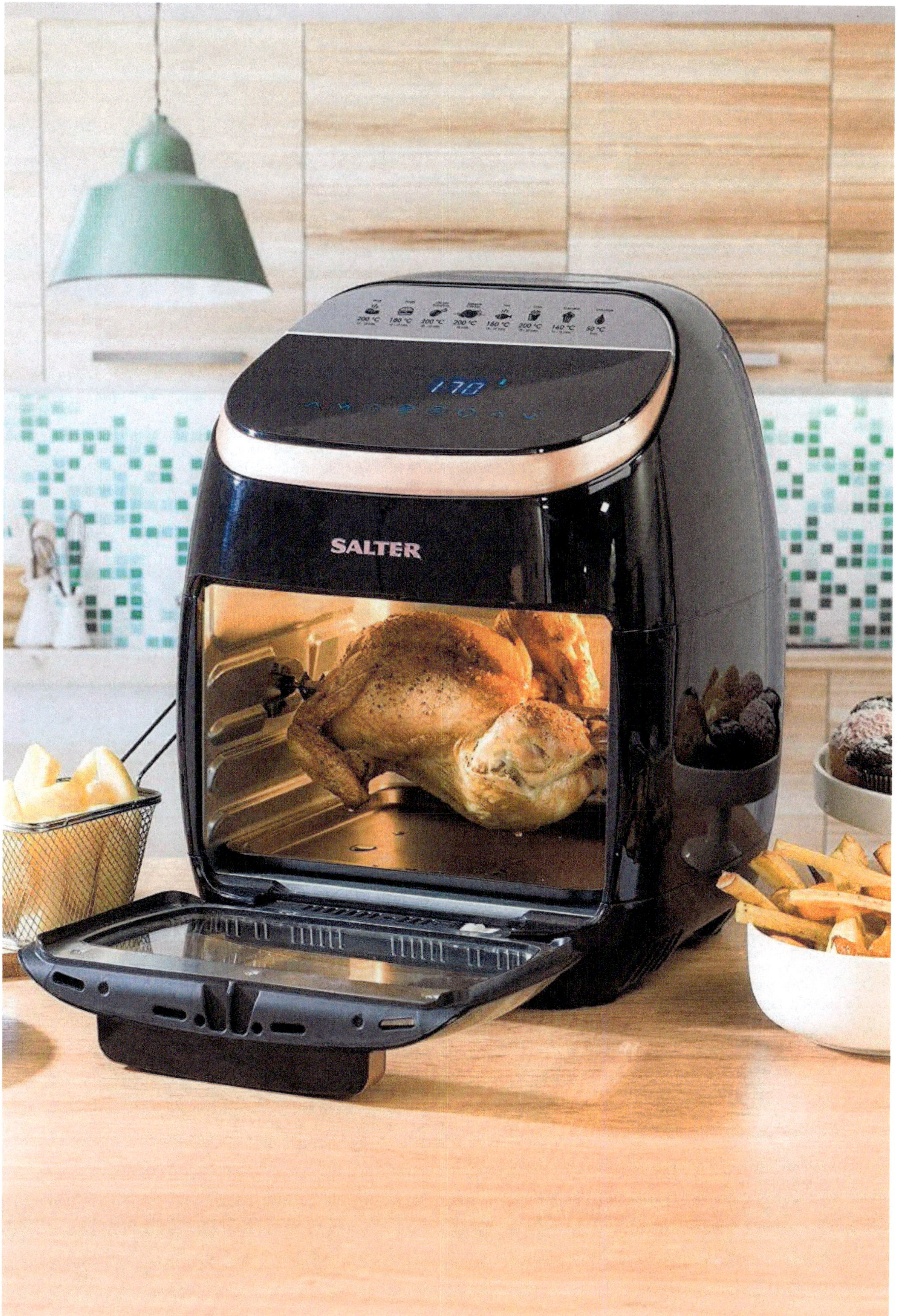
SALTER

Table of Contents

Chapter 1
Basics of UK Tower Air Fryer   1
Safety Measures While Using an Air Fryer   1
You Can Cook Anything   2
UK Tower Air Fryer Saves Money   2

Chapter 2
Staples   3
Polenta with Butter   4
Enchilada Sauce   4
Spice Mix with Cumin   5
Baked Rice   5
Chile Seasoning   6
Asian Dipping Sauce   6
Roasted Mushrooms   7
Simple Teriyaki Sauce   7

Chapter 3
Breakfasts   8
Back Bacon Muffin Sandwiches   9
Coconut Brown Rice Porridge with Dates   9
Corned Beef Hash with Eggs   10
Cornmeal Pancake   10
Crustless Broccoli Quiche   11
Egg and Avocado Burrito   11
Egg Florentine with Spinach   12
Eggy bread Sticks   12
Fried Cheese corn meal   13
Fried Potatoes with Peppers and Onions   13

Chapter 4
Poultry   14
Gai Yang Chicken   15
Smoked Paprika Chicken   15
Almond Meatballs   16
Lemon Chicken Thighs   16
Coriander Chicken Drumsticks   17
Garlic Chicken Wings   17
Sweet Chicken Wings   18
Basil Chicken Wings   18
Coated Chicken   19
Ginger Drumsticks   19
BBQ Wings   20
Asparagus Chicken   20
Provolone Meatballs   21
Nutmeg Chicken Fillets   21
Chicken and Rice Casserole   21
Hazelnut Crusted Chicken   22
Oregano Chicken and Runner Beans   22

Chapter 5
Meats   23
Dijon Mustard Pork Tenderloin   24
Dijon-Lemon Pork Tenderloin   24
Taco Pork Chops with Oregano   25
Chipotle Flank Steak with Oregano   25
Beef and Carrot Meatballs   26
Miso-Sake Marinated Flank Steak   26
Paprika Lamb Chops with Sage   27
Beef Stroganoff with Mushrooms   27
Pork Ribs with Honey-Soy Sauce   28
Beef and Mushroom Meatloaf   28
Beef and Spaghetti marrow Lasagna   29
Cheddar Prosciutto and Potato Salad   29

Chapter 6
Fish and Seafood   30
Deep Fry Squid Rings with Couscous   31
Garlicky Cashew Prawn   31
Prawn with Cauliflower Rice   32
Lemony Prawn with Cucumber   32
Delicious Black Cod with Pecans   33
Salmon and Spring Onion Balls   33
Trout with Yogurt   34
Crisp Rosemary Catfish   34
Grilled tilapia with lemon and pepper   35
Peppery Sardine Cakes   35
Herbed Crab Croquettes   36
Tiger Prawns with Firecracker Sauce   36
Creamy Wild Salmon   37
Spicy Garlicky Chicken with Peppers   37
Authentic Spanish Peppery Pancake   38
French-Style Homemade Ratatouille   38
Grilled Trout with Herbs   38

Chapter 7
Rice and Grains   39
Apple Oat Muffins   40
Cocoa Muffins   40
Scallion Rice Pilaf   41
Curry Basmati Rice   41
Quinoa and Broccoli Cheese Patties   42
Creamy Butter Corn Fritters   42
Honey Prunes Bread Pudding   43
Cherry Cranberry Bread Pudding   43
Almonds Bread Pudding   44
Figs Bread Pudding   44
Cheesy Macaroni   45
Air Fried Butter Toast   45
Chocolate Chips muesli   46
Rice with Scallions   46
Carrot and Green Peas Rice   47
Pumpkin Porridge with Chocolate   47
Chawal ke Pakore with Cheese   48
Rice Cheese Casserole   48
Millet Porridge with Sultanas   49
Creamy Cornbread Casserole   49
Cheesy Carbonara with Pancetta   49

Chapter 8
Side Dishes — 50
- Turmeric Cauliflower Rice — 51
- Mushroom Cakes — 51
- Cauliflower and Tomato Bake — 52
- Turmeric Tofu — 52
- Coconut Chives Sprouts — 53
- Cheesy courgette Tots — 53
- Creamy Broccoli and Cauliflower — 54
- Mushroom Tots — 54
- Mozzarella Risotto — 55
- Creamy Cauliflower Tots — 55
- Spinach Salad — 55

Chapter 9
Starters and Snacks — 56
- Avocado Chips — 57
- Baked Sardines with Tomato Sauce — 57
- Broiled Prosciutto-Wrapped Pears — 58
- Bruschetta with Tomato and Basil — 58
- Browned Ricotta with Capers and Lemon — 59
- Prawn Toasts with Sesame Seeds — 59
- Tuna Melts with Scallions — 60
- Turkey Bacon-Wrapped Dates — 60

Appendix 1 Measurement Conversion Chart — 61
Appendix 2 The Dirty Dozen and Clean Fifteen — 62
Appendix 3 Index — 63

Chapter 1
Basics of UK Tower Air Fryer

Modern air fryers can trace their origin to around 2010. Since then, air fryers have become popular with the masses. In the past few years, during the lockdown, more people took to cooking meals at home, and the popularity of the device has skyrocketed.

While many alliterations of the air fryer exist today, the basic concept has stayed the same. At the heart of it is the use of hot air to cook food. A convection oven uses the same principle. However, it is much smaller and more convenient for cooking small meals for a few people.

During the decade that the air fryer has risen to prominence, one of the biggest names today is the UK Tower Air Fryer. Millions of users respect it. Today, it is part of many kitchens, where tasty meals are prepared at the push of a button.

Safety Measures While Using an Air Fryer

As with any kitchen appliance, there is always a small risk if not handled properly. Thankfully, all UK Tower Air Fryers come with a clear set of instructions that include illustrations. Before using the appliance, one should study and understand the instructions.

To use the air fryer safely, one must understand how it works. The air fryer is fitted with a heating element. When heat is generated, a fan circulates heat all over the food. Circulating heat evenly over the food means cooking requires little to no oil. At the same time, it ensures you can get the same crunchiness as you would when using oil. Unlike oil, food tends to brown evenly, where some foods brown more at the bottom than the rest.

Having understood how it operates, the safety measures are easy to understand. One of the first ones is that the air fryer does not require oil. As such, one should never, under any circumstances, top up the heating basket with oil. Doing so could hamper air circulation and clog up parts with oil.

Another important safety measure is that it should be used in a ventilated area. When using it, ensure that there is enough space around it so that it can ventilate safely. An air fryer should not be placed close to the walls or in the corner. Doing so could reduce its efficiency.

Another issue is the smoke point. Some foods come with a smoke point, which may be indicated on the package. When cooking food, such as bacon, which has a slow smoke point, always set the temperature below this point. If not, it could cause the food to start smoking.

Besides that food, ensure you know the smoke point of the oil you use. Some oils have an extremely low smoke point. Always avoid such oils, or avoid using oil altogether. When the oil smokes, it will cover the heating element, making it less efficient at its role.

Use protective gloves when handling the air fryer basket. Doing so will ensure you never burn your fingers before enjoying tasty meals. The same should go for your countertops. Users should have a hot pad to ensure they are not directly in contact with the basket. With time, it will degrade and have to be replaced.

Another important point is that you should always unplug the appliance when not in use. Since it uses a heating element, there is a real risk of injury if someone handles it without knowing how long ago it was used.

Get yourself a UK Air Fryer today and enjoy some of the tasty recipes below!

You Can Cook Anything

A major fear some people have is what to cook in their UK Tower Air Fryer. Some people fear that they will have to sacrifice their tasty, delicious meals for the speed and convenience it offers. However, that is not true. Anything you can cook in your kitchen can be cooked in the air fryer. Best of all, it can be cooked faster.

You will not have to sacrifice the taste or nutritional value that your family can get. Some people might believe you can only cook French fries on the device. However, that is not true. Anything that needs heat can be cooked inside the appliance.

An air fryer is perfect for cooking your meats. Since it circulates hot air inside the appliance, all the flavors are preserved. You can cook chicken, fish, pork, and even veggie side dishes. For instance, you can cook a tasty zucchini in the air fryer and even some baked goods. If you are looking for inspiration on other meals, you will find plenty of them in this cookbook.

You will love this device if you love your food extra crispy, which most people do. It gives everything you cook an extra crispy skin under the right settings. Whenever you cook inside it, it always comes out flavorful and juicy.

UK Tower Air Fryer Saves Money

A family-sized air fryer uses the latest technology to cook food at the lowest cost possible. In the UK and many places in the world, the price of energy has risen dramatically. Consequently, everyone is interested in saving costs. Experts found that a household could save up to $450 on its cooking bill by using appliances that are more efficient. Regarding saving costs, the Tower Air Fryer is a winner.

Cooking using an air fryer to cook is estimated to cost less than 25 US cents, or a quarter, per meal. When using an electric oven, the rise can quickly rise to slightly over $1 per meal. On that alone, using an air fryer makes sense.

One way that an air fryer helps to cut the cooking cost is the speed at which it cooks. Due to the intensely hot air circulating in the basket, cooking times are often 30 minutes or less for any food that can fit inside it. Everyone has seen their energy bills rise in recent months and anything that helps to reduce the cost is a welcome addition to any kitchen.

Chapter 2
Staples

Polenta with Butter

Prep time: 3 minutes | Cook time: 1 hour 5 minutes | Makes about 4 cups

- 1 cup corn meal or polenta (not instant or quick cook)
- 2 cups chicken or vegetable stock
- 2 cups milk
- 2 tablespoons unsalted butter, cut into 4 pieces
- 1 teaspoon flake salt or ½ teaspoon fine salt

1. Add the corn meal to the baking pan. Stir in the stock, milk, butter, and salt.
2. Select Bake, set the temperature to 160°C, and set the time for 1 hour and 5 minutes. Select Start/Stop to begin preheating.
3. Once the unit has preheated, place the pan on the bake position.
4. After 15 minutes, remove the pan from the oven and stir the polenta. Return the pan to the oven and continue cooking.
5. After 30 minutes, remove the pan again and stir the polenta again. Return the pan to the oven and continue cooking for 15 to 20 minutes, or until the polenta is soft and creamy and the liquid is absorbed.
6. When done, remove the pan from the oven.
7. Serve immediately.

Enchilada Sauce

Prep time: 15 minutes | Cook time: 0 minutes | Makes 2 cups

- 3 large ancho chiles, stems and seeds removed, torn into pieces
- 1½ cups very hot water
- 2 garlic cloves, peeled and lightly smashed
- 2 tablespoons wine vinegar
- 1½ teaspoons sugar
- ½ teaspoon dried oregano
- ½ teaspoon ground cumin
- 2 teaspoons flake salt or 1 teaspoon fine salt

1. Mix together the chile pieces and hot water in a bowl and let stand for 10 to 15 minutes.
2. Pour the chiles and water into a blender jar. Fold in the garlic, vinegar, sugar, oregano, cumin, and salt and blend until smooth.
3. Use immediately.

Spice Mix with Cumin
Prep time: 5 minutes | Cook time: 0 minutes | Makes about 1 tablespoon

- 1 teaspoon smoked paprika
- 1 teaspoon cumin
- ¼ teaspoon turmeric
- ¼ teaspoon flake salt or ⅛ teaspoon fine salt
- ¼ teaspoon cinnamon
- ¼ teaspoon allspice
- ¼ teaspoon red pepper flakes
- ¼ teaspoon freshly ground black pepper

1. Stir together all the ingredients in a small bowl.
2. Use immediately or place in an airtight container in the pantry.

Baked Rice
Prep time: 3 minutes | Cook time: 35 minutes | Makes about 4 cups

- 1 cup long-grain white rice, rinsed and drained
- 1 tablespoon unsalted butter, melted, or 1 tablespoon extra-virgin olive oil
- 2 cups water
- 1 teaspoon flake salt or ½ teaspoon fine salt

1. Add the butter and rice to the baking pan and stir to coat. Pour in the water and sprinkle with the salt. Stir until the salt is dissolved.
2. Select Bake, set the temperature to 160°C, and set the time for 35 minutes. Select Start/Stop to begin preheating.
3. Once the unit has preheated, place the pan on the bake position.
4. After 20 minutes, remove the pan from the oven. Stir the rice. Transfer the pan back to the oven and continue cooking for 10 to 15 minutes, or until the rice is mostly cooked through and the water is absorbed.
5. When done, remove the pan from the oven and cover with tin foil. Let stand for 10 minutes. Using a fork, gently fluff the rice.
6. Serve immediately.

Chile Seasoning

Prep time: 5 minutes | Cook time: 0 minutes | Makes about ¾ cups

- 3 tablespoons ancho chile powder
- 3 tablespoons paprika
- 2 tablespoons dried oregano
- 2 tablespoons freshly ground black pepper
- 2 teaspoons cayenne
- 2 teaspoons cumin
- 1 tablespoon granulated onion
- 1 tablespoon granulated garlic

1. Stir together all the ingredients in a small bowl.
2. Use immediately or place in an airtight container in the pantry.

Asian Dipping Sauce

Prep time: 15 minutes | Cook time: 0 minutes | Makes about 1 cup

- ¼ cup rice vinegar
- ¼ cup hoisin sauce
- ¼ cup low-sodium chicken or vegetable stock
- 3 tablespoons soy sauce
- 1 tablespoon minced or grated ginger
- 1 tablespoon minced or pressed garlic
- 1 teaspoon chili-garlic sauce or sriracha (or more to taste)

1. Stir together all the ingredients in a small bowl, or place in a jar with a tight-fitting lid and shake until well mixed.
2. Use immediately.

Roasted Mushrooms

Prep time: 8 minutes | Cook time: 30 minutes | Makes about 1½ cups

- 1 pound (454 g) button or cremini mushrooms, washed, stems trimmed, and cut into quarters or thick slices
- ¼ cup water
- 1 teaspoon flake salt or ½ teaspoon fine salt
- 3 tablespoons unsalted butter, cut into pieces, or extra-virgin olive oil

1. Place a large piece of tin foil on the sheet pan. Place the mushroom pieces in the middle of the foil. Spread them out into an even layer. Pour the water over them, season with the salt, and add the butter. Wrap the mushrooms in the foil.
2. Select Roast, set the temperature to 160°C, and set the time for 15 minutes. Select Start/Stop to begin preheating.
3. Once the unit has preheated, place the pan on the roast position.
4. After 15 minutes, remove the pan from the oven. Transfer the foil packet to a cutting board and carefully unwrap it. Pour the mushrooms and cooking liquid from the foil onto the sheet pan.
5. Select Roast, set the temperature to 180°C, and set the time for 15 minutes. Place the air fryer basket or wire rack on the roast position. Select Start/Stop to begin.
6. After about 10 minutes, remove the pan from the oven and stir the mushrooms. Return the pan to the oven and continue cooking for anywhere from 5 to 15 more minutes, or until the liquid is mostly gone and the mushrooms start to brown.
7. Serve immediately.

Simple Teriyaki Sauce

Prep time: 5 minutes | Cook time: 0 minutes | Makes ¾ cup

- ½ cup soy sauce
- 3 tablespoons honey
- 1 tablespoon rice wine or dry sherry
- 1 tablespoon rice vinegar
- 2 teaspoons minced fresh ginger
- 2 garlic cloves, smashed

1. Beat together all the ingredients in a small bowl.
2. Use immediately.

Chapter 3
Breakfasts

Back Bacon Muffin Sandwiches

Prep time: 5 minutes | Cook time: 8 minutes | Serves 4

- 4 English muffins, split
- 8 slices back bacon
- 4 slices cheese
- Cooking spray

1. Make the sandwiches: Top each of 4 muffin halves with 2 slices of back bacon, 1 slice of cheese, and finish with the remaining muffin half.
2. Put the sandwiches in the air flow racks and spritz the tops with cooking spray.
3. Slide the racks into the air fryer. Press the Power Button. Cook at 190°C for 8 minutes.
4. Flip the sandwiches halfway through the cooking time.
5. When cooking is complete, remove the racks from the air fryer. Divide the sandwiches among four plates and serve warm.

Coconut Brown Rice Porridge with Dates

Prep time: 5 minutes | Cook time: 23 minutes | Serves 1 or 2

- ½ cup cooked brown rice
- 1 cup tinned coconut milk
- ¼ cup unsweetened desiccated coconut
- ¼ cup packed dark Demerara sugar
- 4 large Medjool dates, pitted and roughly chopped
- ½ teaspoon flaked salt
- ¼ teaspoon ground cardamom
- double cream, for serving (optional)

1. Place all the ingredients except the double cream in a baking pan and stir until blended.
2. Slide the pan into the air fryer. Press the Power Button. Cook at 190°C for 23 minutes.
3. Stir the porridge halfway through the cooking time.
4. When cooked, the porridge will be thick and creamy.
5. Remove from the air fryer and ladle the porridge into bowls.
6. Serve hot with a drizzle of the cream, if desired.

Corned Beef Hash with Eggs

Prep time: 10 minutes | Cook time: 25 minutes | Serves 4

- 2 medium Yukon Gold potatoes, peeled and cut into ¼-inch cubes
- 1 medium onion, chopped
- ⅓ cup diced red bell pepper
- 3 tablespoons vegetable oil
- ½ teaspoon dried thyme
- ½ teaspoon flaked salt, divided
- ½ teaspoon freshly ground black pepper, divided
- ¾ pound (340 g) corned beef, cut into ¼-inch pieces
- 4 large eggs

1. In a large bowl, stir together the potatoes, onion, red pepper, vegetable oil, thyme, ¼ teaspoon of the salt and ¼ teaspoon of the pepper. Spread the vegetable mixture on the sheet pan in an even layer.
2. Slide the pan into the air fryer. Press the Power Button. Cook at 190°C for 25 minutes.
3. After 15 minutes, remove from the air fryer and add the corned beef. Stir the mixture to incorporate the corned beef. Return to the air fryer and continue cooking.
4. After 5 minutes, remove from the air fryer. Using a large spoon, create 4 circles in the hash to hold the eggs. Gently crack an egg into each circle. Season the eggs with the remaining ¼ teaspoon of the salt and ¼ teaspoon of the pepper. Return the pan to the air fryer. Continue cooking for 3 to 5 minutes, depending on how you like your eggs.
5. When cooking is complete, remove from the air fryer. Serve immediately.

Cornmeal Pancake

Prep time: 10 minutes | Cook time: 6 minutes | Serves 4

- 1½ cups yellow cornmeal
- ½ cup plain flour
- 2 tablespoons sugar
- 1 teaspoon salt
- 1 teaspoon baking powder
- 1 cup whole or Semi-Skimmed Milk
- 1 large egg, lightly beaten
- 1 tablespoon butter, melted
- Cooking spray

1. Line the air flow racks with greaseproof paper.
2. Stir together the cornmeal, flour, sugar, salt, and baking powder in a large bowl. Mix in the milk, egg, and melted butter and whisk to combine.
3. Drop tablespoonfuls of the batter onto the greaseproof paper for each pancake. Spray the pancakes with cooking spray. Arrange the pancakes on the air flow racks.
4. Slide the racks into the air fryer. Press the Power Button. Cook at 180°C for 6 minutes.
5. Flip the pancakes and spray with cooking spray again halfway through the cooking time.
6. When cooking is complete, remove the pancakes from the air fryer to a plate.
7. Cool for 5 minutes and serve immediately.

Crustless Broccoli Quiche

Prep time: 5 minutes | Cook time: 10 minutes | Serves 4

- 1 cup broccoli florets
- ¾ cup chopped roasted red peppers
- 1¼ cups grated Fontina cheese
- 6 eggs
- ¾ cup double cream
- ½ teaspoon salt
- Freshly ground black pepper, to taste
- Cooking spray

1. Spritz a baking pan with cooking spray
2. Add the broccoli florets and roasted red peppers to the pan and scatter the grated Fontina cheese on top.
3. In a bowl, beat together the eggs and double cream. Sprinkle with salt and pepper. Pour the egg mixture over the top of the cheese. Wrap the pan in foil.
4. Slide the pan into the air fryer. Press the Power Button. Cook at 160°C for 10 minutes.
5. After 8 minutes, remove from the air fryer. Remove the foil. Return to the air fryer and continue to cook another 2 minutes.
6. When cooked, the quiche should be golden brown.
7. Rest for 5 minutes before cutting into wedges and serve warm.

Egg and Avocado Burrito

Prep time: 10 minutes | Cook time: 4 minutes | Serves 4

- 4 low-sodium whole-wheat flour tortillas

FILLING:
- 1 hard-boiled egg, chopped
- 2 hard-boiled egg whites, chopped
- 1 ripe avocado, peeled, pitted, and chopped
- 1 red bell pepper, chopped
- 1 (1.2-ounce / 34-g) slice low-sodium, low-fat American cheese, torn into pieces
- 3 tablespoons low-sodium salsa, plus additional for serving (optional)

SPECIAL EQUIPMENT:
- 4 Cocktail Sticks (optional), soaked in water for at least 30 minutes

1. Make the filling: Combine the egg, egg whites, avocado, red bell pepper, cheese, and salsa in a medium bowl and stir until blended.
2. Assemble the burritos: Arrange the tortillas on a clean work surface and place ¼ of the prepared filling in the middle of each tortilla, leaving about 1½-inch on each end unfilled. Fold in the opposite sides of each tortilla and roll up. Secure with Cocktail Sticks through the center, if needed.
3. Transfer the burritos to the air flow racks.
4. Slide the racks into the air fryer. Press the Power Button. Cook at 200°C for 4 minutes.
5. When cooking is complete, the burritos should be crisp and golden brown.
6. Allow to cool for 5 minutes and serve with salsa, if desired.

Egg Florentine with Spinach

Prep time: 10 minutes | Cook time: 15 minutes | Serves 4

- 3 cups frozen spinach, thawed and drained
- 2 tablespoons double cream
- ¼ teaspoon flaked salt
- ⅛ teaspoon freshly ground black pepper
- 4 ounces (113 g) Ricotta cheese
- 2 garlic cloves, minced
- ½ cup panko bread crumbs
- 3 tablespoons grated Parmesan cheese
- 2 teaspoons unsalted butter, melted
- 4 large eggs

1. In a medium bowl, whisk together the spinach, double cream, salt, pepper, Ricotta cheese and garlic.
2. In a small bowl, whisk together the bread crumbs, Parmesan cheese and butter. Set aside.
3. Spoon the spinach mixture on the sheet pan and form four even circles.
4. Slide the pan into the air fryer. Press the Power Button. Cook at 190°C for 15 minutes.
5. After 8 minutes, press Cancel and remove the pan. The spinach should be bubbling. With the back of a large spoon, make indentations in the spinach for the eggs. Crack the eggs into the indentations and sprinkle the panko mixture over the surface of the eggs.
6. Return to the air fryer and press Start to continue cooking.
7. When cooking is complete, remove from the air fryer. Serve hot.

Eggy bread Sticks

Prep time: 5 minutes | Cook time: 12 minutes | Serves 4

- 3 slices low-sodium whole-wheat bread, each cut into 4 strips
- 1 tablespoon unsalted butter, melted
- 1 tablespoon 2 percent milk
- 1 tablespoon sugar
- 1 egg, beaten
- 1 egg white
- 1 cup sliced fresh strawberries
- 1 tablespoon freshly squeezed lemon juice

1. Arrange the bread strips on a plate and drizzle with the melted butter.
2. In a bowl, whisk together the milk, sugar, egg and egg white.
3. Dredge the bread strips into the egg mixture and place on a wire rack to let the batter drip off. Arrange half the coated bread strips on the sheet pan.
4. Slide the pan into the air fryer. Press the Power Button. Cook at 190°C for 6 minutes.
5. After 3 minutes, remove from the air fryer. Use a tong to turn the strips over. Rotate the pan and return the pan to the air fryer to continue cooking.
6. When cooking is complete, the strips should be golden brown. Repeat with the remaining strips.
7. In a small bowl, mash the strawberries with a fork and stir in the lemon juice. Serve the Eggy bread sticks with the strawberry sauce.

Fried Cheese corn meal
Prep time: 10 minutes | Cook time: 11 minutes | Serves 4

- ⅔ cup instant corn meal
- 1 teaspoon salt
- 1 teaspoon freshly ground black pepper
- ¾ cup whole or Semi-Skimmed Milk
- 3 ounces (85 g) cream cheese, at room temperature
- 1 large egg, beaten
- 1 tablespoon butter, melted
- 1 cup shredded mild Cheddar cheese
- Cooking spray

1. Mix the corn meal, salt, and black pepper in a large bowl. Add the milk, cream cheese, beaten egg, and melted butter and whisk to combine. Fold in the Cheddar cheese and stir well.
2. Spray a baking pan with cooking spray. Spread the corn meal mixture into the baking pan.
3. Place the pan into the air fryer. Press the Power Button. Cook at 200°C for 11 minutes.
4. Stir the mixture halfway through the cooking time.
5. When done, a knife inserted in the center should come out clean.
6. Rest for 5 minutes and serve warm.

Fried Potatoes with Peppers and Onions
Prep time: 10 minutes | Cook time: 35 minutes | Serves 4

- 1 pound (454 g) red potatoes, cut into ½-inch dices
- 1 large red bell pepper, cut into ½-inch dices
- 1 large green bell pepper, cut into ½-inch dices
- 1 medium onion, cut into ½-inch dices
- 1½ tablespoons extra-virgin olive oil
- 1¼ teaspoons flaked salt
- ¾ teaspoon sweet paprika
- ¾ teaspoon garlic powder
- Freshly ground black pepper, to taste

1. Mix the potatoes, bell peppers, onion, oil, salt, paprika, garlic powder, and black pepper in a large mixing and toss to coat.
2. Transfer the potato mixture to the air flow racks.
3. Slide the racks into the air fryer. Press the Power Button. Cook at 180°C for 35 minutes.
4. Stir the potato mixture three times during cooking.
5. When done, the potatoes should be nicely browned.
6. Remove from the air fryer to a plate and serve warm.

Chapter 4
Poultry

Gai Yang Chicken
Prep time: 15 minutes | Cook time: 65 minutes | Serves 4

- 2-pounds Cornish hens, roughly chopped
- 2 tablespoons Gai yang spices
- 1 tablespoon avocado oil

1. Rub the hens with spices carefully.
2. Then sprinkle the hens with avocado oil and put in the air fryer.
3. Cook the meal at 180°C for 65 minutes.

Smoked Paprika Chicken
Prep time: 10 minutes | Cook time: 20 minutes | Serves 4

- 2-pounds chicken breast, skinless, boneless
- 1 tablespoon smoked paprika
- 1 teaspoon coconut oil, melted
- 1 tablespoon apple cider vinegar

1. In the shallow bowl, mix coconut oil with apple cider vinegar, and smoked paprika.
2. Carefully brush the chicken breast with smoked paprika mixture.
3. Then put the chicken in the air fryer and cook it at 190°C for 20 minutes. Flip the chicken on another side after 10 minutes of cooking.

Almond Meatballs

Prep time: 10 minutes | Cook time: 12 minutes | Serves 6

- 16 oz ground chicken
- ½ cup almond flour
- 1 teaspoon salt
- 1 teaspoon ground black pepper
- 1 tablespoon avocado oil

1. Mix ground chicken with almond flour, salt, and ground black pepper.
2. After this, make the meatballs and put them in the air fryer in one layer.
3. Sprinkle the meatballs with avocado oil and cook at 180°C for 12 minutes.

Lemon Chicken Thighs

Prep time: 5 minutes | Cook time: 30 minutes | Serves 4

- 8 chicken thighs, boneless, skinless
- 1 tablespoon lemon zest, grated
- 2 tablespoons lemon juice
- 1 teaspoon avocado oil
- 1 teaspoon salt

1. Rub the chicken thighs with lemon zest, lemon juice, avocado oil, and salt.
2. Put the chicken thighs in the air fryer basket or wire rack and cook at 180°C for 30 minutes.
3. Flip the chicken thighs on another side after 15 minutes of cooking.

Coriander Chicken Drumsticks

Prep time: 10 minutes | Cook time: 20 minutes | Serves 6

- 6 chicken drumsticks
- 1 tablespoon coconut oil, melted
- 1 tablespoon ground coriander
- 1 teaspoon garlic powder
- ½ teaspoon salt

1. Sprinkle the chicken drumsticks with ground coriander, salt, and garlic powder.
2. Then sprinkle the chicken drumsticks with coconut oil and put it in the air fryer.
3. Cook the meal at 190°C for 20 minutes.

Garlic Chicken Wings

Prep time: 10 minutes | Cook time: 30 minutes | Serves 4

- 2 pounds of chicken wings
- 1 tablespoon coconut oil, softened
- 1 tablespoon garlic powder
- ¼ cup apple cider vinegar

1. Mix chicken wings with coconut oil, garlic powder, and apple cider vinegar.
2. Put them in the air fryer basket or wire rack and cook at 180°C for 30 minutes.

Sweet Chicken Wings

Prep time: 10 minutes | **Cook time:** 16 minutes | **Serves 4**

- 1-pound chicken wings
- 1 tablespoon taco seasonings
- 1 tablespoon Erythritol
- 1 tablespoon coconut oil, melted

1. Mix chicken wings with taco seasonings, Erythritol, and coconut oil.
2. Put the chicken wings in the air fryer basket or wire rack and cook them at 190°C for 16 minutes.

Basil Chicken Wings

Prep time: 5 minutes | **Cook time:** 30 minutes | **Serves 4**

- 2 pounds of chicken wings
- 1 tablespoon dried basil
- 1 teaspoon salt
- 1 tablespoon avocado oil

1. Sprinkle the chicken wings with dried basil, salt, and avocado oil.
2. Put the chicken wings in the air fryer basket or wire rack and cook at 180°C for 30 minutes.

Coated Chicken
Prep time: 15 minutes | Cook time: 20 minutes | Serves 6

- 3-pounds chicken breast, skinless, boneless
- 1 tablespoon coconut shred
- 2 tablespoons scratchings
- 1 teaspoon ground black pepper
- 2 eggs, beaten
- 1 tablespoon avocado oil

1. In the shallow bowl, mix coconut shred with pork rinds, and ground black pepper.
2. Then cut the chicken breasts into 6 servings and dip in the eggs.
3. Coat the chicken in the coconut shred mixture and put it in the air fryer basket or wire rack.
4. Then sprinkle the chicken with avocado oil and cook at 190°C for 20 minutes.

Ginger Drumsticks
Prep time: 5 minutes | Cook time: 20 minutes | Serves 4

- 1 teaspoon ground ginger
- ½ teaspoon ground cinnamon
- 1 tablespoon olive oil
- ½ teaspoon onion powder
- 2-pounds chicken drumsticks

1. Mix the chicken drumsticks with onion powder, olive oil, ground cinnamon, and ground ginger.
2. Put them in the air fryer basket or wire rack and cook at 190°C for 20 minutes.

BBQ Wings

Prep time: 10 minutes | Cook time: 20 minutes | Serves 4

- 2-pound chicken wings
- 1 cup BBQ sauce
- 1 teaspoon olive oil

1. Mix BBQ sauce with olive oil.
2. Brush the chicken wings carefully with the BQ sauce mixture and put it in the air fryer.
3. Cook the chicken wings for 9 minutes per side at 190°C.

Asparagus Chicken

Prep time: 15 minutes | Cook time: 30 minutes | Serves 4

- 1 cup asparagus, chopped
- 1-pound chicken thighs, skinless, boneless
- 1 teaspoon onion powder
- 1 oz scallions, chopped
- 1 tablespoon coconut oil, melted
- 1 teaspoon smoked paprika

1. Mix chicken thighs with onion powder, coconut oil, and smoked paprika.
2. Put the chicken thighs in the air fryer and cook at 200°C for 20 minutes.
3. Then flip the chicken thighs on another side and top with chopped asparagus and scallions.
4. Cook the meal for 5 minutes more.

Provolone Meatballs
Prep time: 10 minutes | Cook time: 12 minutes | Serves 6

- 12 oz ground chicken
- ½ cup coconut flour
- 2 egg whites, whisked
- 1 teaspoon ground black pepper
- 1 egg yolk
- 1 teaspoon salt
- 4 oz Provolone cheese, grated
- 1 teaspoon ground oregano
- ½ teaspoon chili powder
- 1 tablespoon avocado oil

1. In the mixing bowl mix up ground chicken, ground black pepper, egg yolk, salt, Provolone cheese, ground oregano, and chili powder.
2. Stir the mixture until homogenous and make the small meatballs. Dip the meatballs in the whisked egg whites and coat in the coconut flour.
3. Preheat the air fryer to 180°C. Put the chicken meatballs in the air fryer basket or wire rack and cook them for 6 minutes from both sides.

Nutmeg Chicken Fillets
Prep time: 15 minutes | Cook time: 12 minutes | Serves 4

- 16 oz chicken fillets
- 1 teaspoon ground nutmeg
- 1 tablespoon avocado oil
- ½ teaspoon salt

1. Mix ground nutmeg with avocado oil and salt.
2. Then rub the chicken fillet with a nutmeg mixture and put it in the air fryer basket or wire rack.
3. Cook the meal at 200°C for 12 minutes.

Chicken and Rice Casserole
Prep time: 5 minutes | Cook time: 35 minutes | Serves: 4

- 2 cups cauliflower florets, chopped
- A pinch of salt and black pepper
- A drizzle of olive oil
- 6 ounces coconut cream
- 2 tablespoons butter, melted
- 2 teaspoons thyme, chopped
- 1 garlic clove, minced
- 1 tablespoon parsley, chopped
- 4 chicken thighs, boneless and skinless

1. Heat up a pan with the butter over medium heat, add the cream and the other ingredients except the cauliflower, oil and the chicken, whisk, bring to a simmer and cook for 5 minutes.
2. Heat up a pan with the oil over medium-high heat, add the chicken and brown for 2 minutes on each side.
3. In a baking dish that fits the air fryer, mix the chicken with the cauliflower, spread the coconut cream mix all over, put the pan in the machine and cook at 190°C for 20 minutes.
4. Divide between plates and serve hot.

Hazelnut Crusted Chicken

Prep time: 10 minutes | **Cook time:** 10 minutes | **Serves 4**

- 1-pound chicken fillet
- 3 oz hazelnuts, grinded
- 2 egg whites, whisked
- ½ teaspoon ground black pepper
- ½ teaspoon salt
- 1 tablespoon coconut flour
- 1 teaspoon avocad oil

1. Cut the chicken on 4 tenders and sprinkle them with ground black pepper and salt. In the mixing bowl mix up grinded hazelnuts and coconut flour.
2. Then dip the chicken tenders in the whisked egg and coat in the hazelnut mixture. Sprinkle every chicken tender with avocado oil.
3. Preheat the air fryer to 180°C. Place the prepared chicken tenders in the preheated air fryer and cook for 10 minutes.

Oregano Chicken and Runner Beans

Prep time: 5 minutes | **Cook time:** 35 minutes | **Serves 4**

- 4 chicken breasts, skinless, boneless and halved
- 10 ounces chicken stock
- 1 teaspoon oregano, dried
- 10 ounces Runner Beans, trimmed and halved
- 2 tablespoons olive oil
- A pinch of salt and black pepper
- 1 tablespoon parsley, chopped

1. Heat up a pan that fits the air fryer with the oil over medium-high heat, add the chicken and brown for 2 minutes on each side.
2. Add the remaining ingredients, toss a bit, put the pan in the machine and cook at 190°C for 30 minutes. Divide everything between plates and serve.

Chapter 5
Meats

Dijon Mustard Pork Tenderloin
Prep time: 5 minutes | Cook time: 12 minutes | Serves 6

- 2 large egg whites
- 1½ tablespoons Dijon mustard
- 2 cups crushed pretzel crumbs
- 1½ pounds (680 g) pork tenderloin, cut into ¼-pound (113-g) sections
- Cooking spray

1. Preheat the air fryer to 190°C. Spritz the baking pan with cooking spray.
2. Whisk the egg whites with Dijon mustard in a bowl until bubbly. Pour the pretzel crumbs in a separate bowl.
3. Dredge the pork tenderloin in the egg white mixture and press to coat. Shake the excess off and roll the tenderloin over the pretzel crumbs.
4. Arrange the well-coated pork tenderloin in batches in a single layer in the pan and spritz with cooking spray.
5. Bake for 12 minutes or until the pork is golden brown and crispy. Flip the pork halfway through. Repeat with remaining pork sections.
6. Serve immediately.

Dijon-Lemon Pork Tenderloin
Prep time: 10 minutes | Cook time: 30 minutes | Serves 4 to 6

- ¼ cup olive oil
- ¼ cup soy sauce
- ¼ cup freshly squeezed lemon juice
- 1 garlic clove, minced
- 1 tablespoon Dijon mustard
- 1 teaspoon salt
- ½ teaspoon freshly ground black pepper
- 2 pounds (907 g) pork tenderloin

1. In a large mixing bowl, make the marinade: Mix the olive oil, soy sauce, lemon juice, minced garlic, Dijon mustard, salt, and pepper. Reserve ¼ cup of the marinade.
2. Put the tenderloin in a large bowl and pour the remaining marinade over the meat. Cover and marinate in the refrigerator for about 1 hour.
3. Preheat the air fryer to 200°C.
4. Put the marinated pork tenderloin into the baking pan. Bake for 10 minutes. Flip the pork and baste it with half of the reserved marinade. Bake for 10 minutes more.
5. Flip the pork, then baste with the remaining marinade. Bake for another 10 minutes, for a total cooking time of 30 minutes.
6. Serve immediately.

Taco Pork Chops with Oregano
Prep time: 5 minutes | Cook time: 18 minutes | Serves 2

- ¼ teaspoon dried oregano
- 1½ teaspoons taco seasoning mix
- 2 (4-ounce / 113-g) boneless pork chops
- 2 tablespoons unsalted butter, divided

1. Preheat the air fryer to 200°C.
2. Combine the dried oregano and taco seasoning in a small bowl and rub the mixture into the pork chops. Brush the chops with 1 tablespoon butter.
3. In the air fryer, bake the chops for 18 minutes, turning them over halfway through to bake on the other side.
4. When the chops are a brown colour, check the internal temperature has reached 60°C and remove from the air fryer. Serve with a garnish of remaining butter.

Chipotle Flank Steak with Oregano
Prep time: 5 minutes | Cook time: 18 minutes | Serves 4

- 3 chipotle peppers in adobo, chopped
- ⅓ cup chopped fresh oregano
- ⅓ cup chopped fresh parsley
- 4 cloves garlic, minced
- Juice of 2 limes
- 1 teaspoon ground cumin seeds
- ⅓ cup olive oil
- 1 to 1½ pounds (454 g to 680 g) flank steak
- Salt, to taste

1. Combine the chipotle, oregano, parsley, garlic, lime juice, cumin, and olive oil in a large bowl. Stir to mix well.
2. Dunk the flank steak in the mixture and press to coat well. Wrap the bowl in plastic and marinate under room temperature for at least 30 minutes.
3. Preheat the air fryer to 200°C.
4. Discard the marinade and place the steak in the preheated air fryer. Sprinkle with salt.
5. Bake for 18 minutes or until the steak is medium-rare or it reaches your desired doneness. Flip the steak halfway through the cooking time.
6. Remove the steak from the air fryer and slice to serve.

Beef and Carrot Meatballs

Prep time: 10 minutes | **Cook time:** 14 minutes | **Serves 8**

- 1 pound (454 g) minced beef
- 1 egg, beaten
- 2 carrots, shredded
- 2 bread slices, crumbled
- 1 small onion, minced
- ½ teaspoons garlic salt
- Pepper and salt, to taste
- 1 cup tomato sauce
- 2 cups pasta sauce

1. Preheat the air fryer to 200°C.
2. In a bowl, combine the minced beef, egg, carrots, crumbled bread, onion, garlic salt, pepper and salt.
3. Divide the mixture into equal amounts and shape each one into a small meatball.
4. Put them in the baking pan and bake for 8 minutes.
5. Transfer the meatballs to an air fryer-safe dish and top with the tomato sauce and pasta sauce.
6. Set the dish into the air fryer and allow to bake at 180°C for 6 more minutes. Serve hot.

Miso-Sake Marinated Flank Steak

Prep time: 5 minutes | **Cook time:** 15 minutes | **Serves 4**

- ¾ pound (340 g) flank steak
- 1½ tablespoons sake
- 1 tablespoon brown miso paste
- 1 teaspoon honey
- 2 cloves garlic, pressed
- 1 tablespoon olive oil

1. Put all the ingredients in a Ziploc bag. Shake to cover the steak well with the seasonings and refrigerate for at least 1 hour.
2. Preheat the air fryer to 200°C. Coat all sides of the steak with cooking spray. Put the steak in the baking pan.
3. Bake for 15 minutes, turning the steak twice during the cooking time, then serve immediately.

Paprika Lamb Chops with Sage

Prep time: 5 minutes | Cook time: 30 minutes | Serves 4

- 1 cup plain flour
- 2 teaspoons dried sage leaves
- 2 teaspoons garlic powder
- 1 tablespoon mild paprika
- 1 tablespoon salt
- 4 (6-ounce / 170-g) bone-in lamb shoulder chops, fat trimmed
- Cooking spray

1. Preheat the air fryer to 200°C and spritz the baking pan with cooking spray.
2. Combine the flour, sage leaves, garlic powder, paprika, and salt in a large bowl. Stir to mix well. Dunk in the lamb chops and toss to coat well.
3. Arrange the lamb chops in a single layer in the pan and spritz with cooking spray. Bake for 30 minutes or until the chops are golden brown and reaches your desired doneness. Flip the chops halfway through.
4. Serve immediately.

Beef Stroganoff with Mushrooms

Prep time: 15 minutes | Cook time: 17 minutes | Serves 4

- 1 pound (454 g) beef steak, thinly sliced
- 8 ounces (227 g) mushrooms, sliced
- 1 whole onion, chopped
- 2 cups beef broth
- 1 cup Soured cream
- 4 tablespoons butter, melted
- 2 cups cooked egg noodles

1. Preheat the air fryer to 200°C.
2. Combine the mushrooms, onion, beef broth, Soured cream and butter in a bowl until well blended. Add the beef steak to another bowl.
3. Spread the mushroom mixture over the steak and let marinate for 10 minutes.
4. Pour the marinated steak in a baking pan and bake in the preheated air fryer for 17 minutes, or until the steak is browned and the vegetables are tender.
5. Serve hot with the cooked egg noodles.

Pork Ribs with Honey-Soy Sauce
Prep time: 5 minutes | Cook time: 36 minutes | Serves 4

- ¼ cup soy sauce
- ¼ cup honey
- 1 teaspoon garlic powder
- 1 teaspoon ground dried ginger
- 4 (8-ounce / 227-g) boneless country-style pork ribs
- Cooking spray

1. Preheat the air fryer to 190°C. Spritz the baking pan with cooking spray.
2. Make the teriyaki sauce: Combine the soy sauce, honey, garlic powder, and ginger in a bowl. Stir to mix well.
3. Brush the ribs with half of the teriyaki sauce, then arrange the ribs in the pan. Spritz with cooking spray. You may need to work in batches to avoid overcrowding.
4. Bake for 36 minutes or until the internal temperature of the ribs reaches at least 60°C. Brush the ribs with remaining teriyaki sauce and flip halfway through.
5. Serve immediately.

Beef and Mushroom Meatloaf
Prep time: 10 minutes | Cook time: 25 minutes | Serves 4

- 1 pound (454 g) minced beef
- 1 egg, beaten
- 1 mushrooms, sliced
- 1 tablespoon thyme
- 1 small onion, chopped
- 3 tablespoons bread crumbs
- Ground black pepper, to taste

1. Preheat the air fryer to 200°C.
2. Put all the ingredients into a large bowl and combine entirely.
3. Transfer the meatloaf mixture into the loaf pan.
4. Bake for 25 minutes. Slice up before serving.

Beef and Spaghetti marrow Lasagna

Prep time: 5 minutes | Cook time: 1 hour 15 minutes | Serves 6

- 2 large spaghetti marrow, cooked (about 2¾ pounds / 1.2 kg)
- 4 pounds (1.8 kg) minced beef
- 1 (2½-pound / 1.1-kg) large jar Marinara sauce
- 25 slices Mozzarella cheese
- 30 ounces whole-milk ricotta cheese

1. Preheat the air fryer to 190°C.
2. Slice the spaghetti marrow and place it face down inside a baking dish. Fill with water until covered.
3. Bake in the preheated air fryer for 45 minutes until skin is soft.
4. Sear the minced beef in a frying pan over medium-high heat for 5 minutes or until browned, then add the marinara sauce and heat until warm. Set aside.
5. Scrape the flesh off the cooked marrow to resemble strands of spaghetti.
6. Layer the lasagna in a large greased pan in alternating layers of spaghetti marrow, beef sauce, Mozzarella, ricotta. Repeat until all the ingredients have been used.
7. Bake for 30 minutes and serve!

Cheddar Prosciutto and Potato Salad

Prep time: 10 minutes | Cook time: 8 minutes | Serves 8

SALAD:
- 4 pounds (1.8 kg) potatoes, boiled and cubed
- 15 slices prosciutto, diced
- 2 cups shredded Cheddar cheese

DRESSING:
- 15 ounces (425 g) Soured cream
- 2 tablespoons mayonnaise
- 1 teaspoon salt
- 1 teaspoon black pepper
- 1 teaspoon dried basil

1. Preheat the air fryer to 190°C.
2. Put the potatoes, prosciutto, and Cheddar in a baking dish. Put it in the air fryer and bake for 8 minutes.
3. In a separate bowl, mix the Soured cream, mayonnaise, salt, pepper, and basil using a whisk.
4. Coat the salad with the dressing and serve.

Chapter 6
Fish and Seafood

Deep Fry Squid Rings with Couscous
Prep time: 10 minutes | Cook time: 22 minutes | Serves 4

- 1 cup couscous
- 1 pound (454 g) squid rings
- 2 large eggs
- ½ cup plain flour
- ½ cup semolina
- 1 teaspoon ground coriander seeds
- 1 teaspoon cayenne pepper
- Salt and black pepper to taste
- 4 lemon wedges to garnish

1. Place the couscous in a large bowl and cover with boiling water. Season with salt and pepper and stir. Cover and set aside for 5 to 7 minutes until the water is absorbed.
2. Preheat air fryer to 200°C. Beat the eggs in a bowl. In another bowl, combine the flour, semolina, ground coriander, cayenne pepper, salt, and pepper.
3. Dip the squid rings in the eggs first, then in the flour mixture, and place them in the greased frying basket.
4. Air Fry for 15 minutes, until golden brown, shaking once. Transfer the couscous to a large platter and arrange the squid rings on top. Serve.

Garlicky Cashew Prawn
Prep time: 10 minutes | Cook time: 30 minutes | Serves 4

- 3 ounces (85 g) cashews, chopped
- 1 tablespoon fresh rosemary, chopped
- 1½ pounds (680 g) Prawn
- 1 garlic clove, minced
- 1 tablespoon breadcrumbs
- 1 egg, beaten
- 1 tablespoon olive oil
- Salt and black pepper to taste

1. Preheat air fryer to 160°C. Combine olive oil with garlic and brush onto the Prawn. Combine rosemary, cashews, and crumbs in a bowl.
2. Dip Prawn in the egg and coat it in the cashew mixture. Place in the frying basket and bake for 25 minutes.
3. Increase the temperature to 200°C and cook for 5 more minutes. Cover with a foil and let sit for a couple of minutes before serving.

Prawn with Cauliflower Rice
Prep time: 10 minutes | **Cook time:** 42 minutes | **Serves 2**

- 1 aubergine, large
- ¼ teaspoon salt, divided
- cooking spray
- ½ pound (226 g) Prawn, peeled & deveined
- ¼ teaspoon black pepper, ground
- 1 cup cauliflower, riced
- 1 scallion, without the head, finely chopped
- ¼ cup greek yogurt, plain, low fat
- ¼ cup parmesan cheese, shredded

1. Wash aubergine and cut into 4 rounds. Remove the flesh and make it into a cup shape.
2. Chop the flesh and keep ready to use. Rub inside with half portion of the salt.
3. Put in the air fryer grill tray and bake for 18 minutes at 200°C.
4. After baking, keep it aside. Now season the Prawn with pepper and the remaining salt. Place it in the air fryer grill tray and spray some cooking oil.
5. Broil it for 5 minutes by flipping sides halfway through the cooking, until it turns to pink. After that, remove and keep it aside.
6. In the air fry tray, put the chopped aubergine flesh, cauliflower rice, scallions, and air fry or 3 to 4 minutes until they become tender. Transfer the air fried veggies into a bowl and add the fried Prawns into it. Add yogurt and combine to mix.
7. Now scoop the mix into the aubergine cup. Top it with grated parmesan cheese.
8. Put it in the air fryer baking grill and bake for 15 minutes at 200°C. Serve hot.

Lemony Prawn with Cucumber
Prep time: 10 minutes | **Cook time:** 20 minutes | **Serves 2**

- 15 ounces (425 g) Cooked Prawns
- 1 cup Cucumber sliced
- 1½ teaspoon Olive oil
- 1 tablespoon Cajun seasoning
- 4 ounces (113 g) Avocado sauce
- ½ cup Onion, green, sliced
- 2 tablespoon Coriander, fresh, finely chopped
- 1 tablespoon Lemon juice
- ¼ teaspoon Salt
- ½ teaspoon Cayenne

1. In a large bowl, put the Prawns, olive oil, and toss well.
2. Place the marinated Prawns in the air fryer.
3. Set the temperature to 200°C and air fry for 12 minutes by intermittently shaking the air fryer basket or wire rack.
4. For preparing the sauce, in a large bowl, combine all the sauce ingredients.
5. On a serving plate, arrange the sliced cucumber and top it with avocado sauce.
6. On top, place the air fried Prawns.
7. Enjoy the Prawn bites.

Delicious Black Cod with Pecans
Prep time: 5 minutes | Cook time: 15 minutes | Serves 2

- 2 black cod fillets
- Salt and black pepper to taste
- 1 small fennel bulb, sliced
- ½ cup pecans
- 2 teaspoon white balsamic vinegar
- 2 tablespoon olive oil

1. Preheat air fryer to 200°C. Season fillets with salt and black pepper and drizzle some olive oil. Place in the air fryer basket or wire rack and Air Fry for 10 minutes, flipping once halfway through. Remove to a plate. Add pecans and fennel slices to a baking dish.
2. Drizzle with olive oil and season with salt and black pepper. Transfer the dish to the fryer and Bake for 5 minutes. When ready, add balsamic vinegar and olive oil to the mixture, season with salt and black pepper. Pour over the black cod and serve.

Salmon and Spring Onion Balls
Prep time: 10 minutes | Cook time: 10 minutes | Serves 2

- 1 cup tinned salmon
- ¼ celery stalk, chopped
- 1 spring onion, sliced
- 4 tablespoon wheat germs
- 2 tablespoon olive oil
- 1 large egg
- 1 tablespoon fresh dill, chopped
- ½ teaspoon garlic powder

1. Preheat air fryer to 200°C. In a large bowl, mix tinned salmon, egg, celery, onion, dill, and garlic.
2. Shape the mixture into balls and roll them in wheat germ. Carefully flatten and place in them the greased air fryer basket or wire rack.
3. Air Fry for 8 to 10 minutes, flipping once halfway through until golden. Serve warm.

Trout with Yogurt
Prep time: 5 minutes | Cook time: 14 minutes | Serves 4

- 4 trout pieces
- 2 tablespoon olive oil
- Salt to taste
- ½ cup greek yogurt
- 2 garlic cloves, minced
- 2 tablespoon fresh dill, finely chopped

1. Preheat air fryer to 190°C. Drizzle the trout with olive oil and season with salt. Place the seasoned trout into the frying basket and Air Fry for 12 to 14 minutes, flipping once.
2. In a bowl, mix Greek yogurt, garlic, chopped dill, and salt. Top the trout with the dill sauce and serve.

Crisp Rosemary Catfish
Prep time: 5 minutes | Cook time: 15 minutes | Serves 4

- 4 catfish fillets
- ¼ cup seasoned fish fry
- 1 tablespoon olive oil
- 1 tablespoon fresh rosemary, chopped

1. Preheat air fryer to 200°C. Add the seasoned fish fry and the fillets to a large Ziploc bag; massage well to coat. Place the fillets in the greased frying basket and Air Fry for 10 to 12 minutes.
2. Flip the fillets and cook for 2 to 3 more minutes until crispy. Top with freshly chopped rosemary and serve.

Grilled tilapia with lemon and pepper
Prep time: 5 minutes | Cook time: 12 minutes | Serves 4

- 1 pound (454 g) tilapia fillets
- 1 teaspoon old bay seasoning
- 2 tablespoon rapeseed oil
- 2 tablespoon lemon pepper
- Salt to taste
- 2 butter buds

1. Preheat air fryer to 200°C. Drizzle rapeseed oil over tilapia.
2. In a bowl, mix salt, lemon pepper, butter buds, and old bay seasoning; spread on the fish. Place the fillets in the fryer to Air Fry for 10 to 12 minutes, turning once, until crispy. Serve with green salad.

Peppery Sardine Cakes
Prep time: 5 minutes | Cook time: 8 minutes | Serves 4

- 2 (4-oz/ 113 g) tins Sardines, chopped
- 2 eggs, beaten
- ½ cup breadcrumbs
- ⅓ cup spring onions, finely chopped
- 2 tablespoon fresh parsley, chopped
- 1 tablespoon mayonnaise
- 1 teaspoon sweet chili sauce
- ½ teaspoon paprika
- Salt and black pepper to taste
- 2 tablespoon olive oil

1. In a bowl, add Sardines, eggs, breadcrumbs, spring onions, parsley, mayonnaise, chili sauce, paprika, salt, and black pepper.
2. Mix well with hands. Shape into 8 cakes and brush them lightly with olive oil. Air Fry in the fryer for 8 minutes at 200°C, shaking once halfway through cooking. Serve warm.

Herbed Crab Croquettes
Prep time: 15 minutes | Cook time: 10 minutes | Serves 4

- 1½ pounds (680 g) lump crab meat
- ⅓ cup Soured cream
- ⅓ cup mayonnaise
- 1 red pepper, finely chopped
- ⅓ cup red onion, chopped
- ½ celery stalk, chopped
- 1 teaspoon fresh tarragon, chopped
- 1 teaspoon fresh chives, chopped
- 1 teaspoon fresh parsley, chopped
- 1 teaspoon cayenne pepper
- 1 ½ cups breadcrumbs
- 2 teaspoon olive oil
- 1 cup flour
- 3 eggs, beaten
- Salt to taste
- Lemon wedges to serve

1. Heat olive oil in a frying pan over medium heat and sauté red pepper, onion, and celery for 5 minutes or until sweaty and translucent. Turn off the heat. Pour the breadcrumbs and salt on a plate.
2. In 2 separate bowls, add the flour and beaten eggs, respectively, set aside. In a separate bowl, add crabmeat, mayo, Soured cream, tarragon, chives, parsley, cayenne pepper, and vegetable sauteed mix.
3. Form bite-sized oval balls from the mixture and place them onto a plate. Preheat air fryer to 200°C. Dip each crab meatball in the beaten eggs and press them in the breadcrumb mixture.
4. Place the croquettes in the greased fryer basket without overcrowding. Cook for 10 minutes until golden brown, shaking once halfway through. Serve hot with lemon wedges.

Tiger Prawns with Firecracker Sauce
Prep time: 10 minutes | Cook time: 10 minutes | Serves 4

- 1 pound (454 g) tiger prawns, peeled
- Salt and black pepper to taste
- 2 eggs
- ½ cup flour
- ¼ cup sesame seeds
- ¾ cup seasoned breadcrumbs
- Firecracker sauce:
- ⅓ cup Soured cream
- 2 tablespoon buffalo sauce
- ¼ cup spicy ketchup
- 1 green onion, chopped

1. Preheat air fryer to 200°C. Beat the eggs in a bowl with salt. In another bowl, mix breadcrumbs with sesame seeds.
2. In a third bowl, mix flour with salt and pepper. Dip prawns in the flour and then in the eggs, and finally in the crumbs.
3. Spray with cooking spray and Air Fry for 10 minutes, flipping once. Meanwhile, mix well all thee sauce ingredients, except for green onion in a bowl.
4. Serve the prawns with firecracker sauce and scatter with freshly chopped spring onions.

Creamy Wild Salmon
Prep time: 5 minutes | Cook time: 15 minutes | Serves 2

- 4 Alaskan wild salmon fillets
- 2 teaspoon olive oil Salt to taste
- ½ cup double cream
- ½ cup milk
- 2 tablespoon fresh parsley, chopped

1. Preheat air fryer to 190°C. Drizzle the fillets with olive oil, and season with salt and black pepper.
2. Place salmon in the frying basket and Bake for 15 minutes, turning once until tender and crispy. In a bowl, mix milk, parsley, salt, and whipped cream. Serve the salmon with the sauce

Spicy Garlicky Chicken with Peppers
Prep time: 10 minutes | Cook time: 10 minutes | Serves 4

- 1 cup breadcrumbs
- ½ cup yogurt
- 1 pound (454 g) chicken breasts, cut into strips
- ½ teaspoon red chili pepper
- 1 tablespoon chili sauce
- 2 eggs, beaten
- 1 teaspoon sweet paprika
- 1 teaspoon garlic powder

1. Preheat air fryer to 200°C. Whisk eggs with the chili sauce and yogurt. In a shallow bowl, combine the breadcrumbs, paprika, cayenne pepper, and garlic powder. Line a baking dish with greaseproof paper.
2. Dip the chicken in the egg/yogurt mixture first, and then coat with breadcrumbs. Arrange on the sheet and Bake in the air fryer for 8 to 10 minutes. Flip the chicken over and bake for 6-8 more minutes. Serve.

Authentic Spanish Peppery Pancake
Prep time: 10 minutes | Cook time: 38 minutes | Serves 4

- 1 pound (454 g) waxy potatoes, into bite-size chunks
- 4 tablespoon olive oil
- 1 teaspoon smoked paprika
- 1 shallot, chopped
- 2 tomatoes, chopped
- 1 tablespoon tomato purée
- 1 tablespoon flour
- 2 tablespoon sriracha hot chili sauce
- 1 teaspoon sugar
- 2 tablespoon fresh parsley, chopped
- Salt to taste

1. Heat 2 tablespoon of the olive oil in a frying pan over medium heat and sauté the shallot for 3 minutes until fragrant.
2. Stir in the flour for 2 more minutes. Add in the remaining ingredients and 1 cup of water. Bring to a boil, reduce the heat, and simmer for 6 to 8 minutes until the sauce becomes pulpy.
3. Remove to a food processor and blend until smooth. Let cool completely. Preheat air fryer to 200°C.
4. Coat potatoes with the remaining olive oil and Air Fry in the fryer for 20 to 25 minutes, shaking once halfway through. Sprinkle with salt and spoon over the sauce to serve. enjoy!

French-Style Homemade Ratatouille
Prep time: 10 minutes | Cook time: 15 minutes | Serves 2

- 2 tablespoon olive oil
- 2 Roma tomatoes, thinly sliced
- 2 garlic cloves, minced
- 1 courgette, thinly sliced
- 2 yellow bell peppers, sliced
- 1 tablespoon vinegar
- 2 tablespoon herbs de Provence
- Salt and black pepper to taste

1. Preheat air fryer to 200°C. Place all ingredients in a bowl. Season with salt and pepper and stir to coat.
2. Arrange them on a baking dish and place them inside the air fryer. Bake for 15 minutes. Serve warm. enjoy!

Grilled Trout with Herbs
Prep time: 10 minutes | Cook time: 14 minutes | Serves 2

- 2 whole trout, scaled and cleaned
- ¼ bulb fennel, sliced
- ½ brown onion, sliced
- 1 tablespoon fresh parsley, chopped
- 1 tablespoon fresh dill, chopped
- 1 tablespoon olive oil
- 1 lemon, sliced
- Salt and black pepper to taste

1. In a bowl, add the onion, parsley, dill, fennel, and garlic. Mix and drizzle with olive oil. Preheat air fryer to 180°C.
2. Open the cavity of the fish and fill with the fennel mixture. Wrap the fish completely in greaseproof paper and then in foil.
3. Place the fish in the frying basket and Bake for 14 minutes. Remove the paper and foil and top with lemon slices to serve.

Chapter 7
Rice and Grains

Apple Oat Muffins

Prep time: 8 minutes | Cook time: 15 minutes | Serves 6

- ½ cups self-raising flour
- ½ cup rolled oats
- ½ cup agave syrup
- ¼ teaspoon grated nutmeg
- ½ teaspoon cinnamon powder
- A pinch of coarse salt
- ½ cup milk
- ¼ cup coconut oil, room temperature
- 2 eggs
- 1 teaspoon coconut extract
- 1 cup cored and chopped apples

1. Mix all ingredients in a bowl.
2. Scrape the batter into silicone baking molds; place them in the baking dish.
3. Place the baking dish in the air fryer basket or wire rack. and bake in the preheated instant pot at 160°C for 15 minutes or until a tester comes out dry and clean.
4. Allow the muffins to cool before unmolding and serving.

Cocoa Muffins

Prep time: 5 minutes | Cook time: 15 minutes | Serves 6

- ½ cup coconut flour
- ½ cup plain flour
- ½ cup cocoa powder
- ½ cup Demerara sugar
- ½ teaspoon baking powder
- A pinch of sea salt
- A pinch of grated nutmeg
- 1 tablespoon instant coffee granules
- ½ cup milk
- 2 eggs, whisked
- ½ teaspoon vanilla extract

1. Mix all ingredients until well combined; then, divide the batter evenly between silicone baking molds; place them in the baking dish.
2. Place the baking dish in the air fryer basket or wire rack. and bake in the preheated instant pot at 170°C for 15 minutes or until a tester comes out dry and clean.
3. Allow the muffins to cool before unmolding and serving. Bon appétit!

Scallion Rice Pilaf

Prep time: 10 minutes | Cook time: 10 minutes | Serves 4

- 1½ cups cooked multigrain rice
- 1 cup vegetable broth
- ½ cup thinly sliced scallions
- 1 tablespoon chopped fresh parsley
- 1 tablespoon chopped fresh Coriander
- 2 tablespoons olive oil
- Sea salt and cayenne pepper, to taste
- 1 teaspoon garlic powder

1. Thoroughly combine all ingredients in a lightly greased baking dish.
2. Place the baking dish in the air fryer basket or wire rack. and bake in the preheated instant pot at 180°C for 10 minutes or until cooked through.
3. Bon appétit!

Curry Basmati Rice

Prep time: 10 minutes | Cook time: 10 minutes | Serves 4

- 3 tablespoons olive oil
- 3 cloves garlic, chopped
- 1 large onion, peeled and chopped
- 1 sprigs fresh curry leaves, chopped
- 2 cups basmati rice, cooked
- 1 teaspoon cayenne pepper
- flake salt and ground black pepper, to taste

1. Thoroughly combine all ingredients in a lightly greased baking dish. Pour 1 cup of boiling water over the rice.
2. Place the baking dish in the air fryer basket or wire rack. and bake in the preheated instant pot at 180°C for 10 minutes or until cooked through.
3. Bon appétit!

Quinoa and Broccoli Cheese Patties
Prep time: 15 minutes | Cook time: 15 minutes | Serves 4

- 2 cups quinoa, cooked
- 2 eggs, whisked
- 1 small onion, chopped
- 2 garlic cloves, minced
- 1 cup chopped broccoli
- ½ cup bread crumbs
- ½ cup grated Parmesan cheese
- 1 tablespoon chopped fresh Italian herbs
- Sea salt and ground black pepper, to taste

1. Mix all ingredients until everything is well combined. Form the mixture into patties. Transfer to the air fryer basket or wire rack.
2. and air fry in the preheated instant pot at 190°C for 15 minutes. Flip the patties halfway through.
3. Bon appétit!

Creamy Butter Corn Fritters
Prep time: 5 minutes | Cook time: 15 minutes | Serves 4

- 1 cup tinned and creamed corn kernels
- 1 cup whole-wheat flour
- 1 teaspoon baking powder
- 2 eggs, whisked
- ½ cup double cream
- 2 tablespoons butter

1. Mix all ingredients until everything is well combined. Form the mixture into patties. Transfer to the air fryer basket or wire rack.
2. and air fry in the preheated instant pot at 190°C for 15 minutes. Flip the fritters halfway through.
3. Bon appétit!

Honey Prunes Bread Pudding

Prep time: 10 minutes | Cook time: 20 minutes | Serves 5

- 8 slices bread, cubed
- 1 cup coconut milk
- ¼ cup coconut oil
- 1 egg, beaten
- ¼ cup honey
- ½ teaspoon ground cinnamon
- ¼ teaspoon ground cloves
- A pinch of flaked salt
- ½ cup pitted and chopped prunes

1. Place the bread cubes in a lightly greased baking dish.
2. In a mixing bowl, thoroughly combine the milk, coconut oil, egg, honey, cinnamon, cloves, and salt.
3. Pour the custard mixture over the bread cubes. Fold in the prunes and set aside for 15 minutes to soak.
4. Preheat the air fryer to .
5. Place the baking dish in the air fryer basket or wire rack. and bake in the preheated instant pot at 180°C for 20 minutes or until the custard is set but still a little wobbly.
6. Bon appétit!

Cherry Cranberry Bread Pudding

Prep time: 5 minutes | Cook time: 20 minutes | Serves 6

- 2 cups cubed sweet raisin bread
- 2 eggs, whisked
- 1 cup milk
- ½ teaspoon vanilla extract
- ¼ cup agave syrup
- ¼ cup dried cherries
- ¼ cup dried cranberries

1. Place the bread cubes in a lightly greased baking dish.
2. In a mixing bowl, thoroughly combine the remaining ingredients.
3. Pour the egg mixture over the bread cubes; set aside for 15 minutes to soak.
4. Place the baking dish in the air fryer basket or wire rack. and bake in the preheated instant pot at 180°C for 20 minutes or until the custard is set but still a little wobbly.
5. Serve at room temperature. Bon appétit!

Almonds Bread Pudding

Prep time: 8 minutes | **Cook time:** 20 minutes | **Serves 6**

- 2 cups cubed Brioche bread
- ½ teaspoon cinnamon powder
- 4 tablespoons Demerara sugar
- 2 eggs, whisked
- 2 tablespoons coconut oil
- 1 cup eggnog
- ½ cup chopped almonds

1. Place the bread cubes in a lightly greased baking dish.
2. In a mixing bowl, thoroughly combine the remaining ingredients.
3. Pour the custard mixture over the bread cubes. Set aside for 15 minutes to soak.
4. Place the baking dish in the air fryer basket or wire rack. and bake in the preheated instant pot at 180°C for 20 minutes or until the custard is set but still a little wobbly.
5. Bon appétit!

Figs Bread Pudding

Prep time: 10 minutes | **Cook time:** 20 minutes | **Serves 5**

- 8 slices bread, cubed
- 1 cup milk
- 2 eggs, beaten
- ¼ cup Demerara sugar
- 2 ounces (57 g) dried figs, chopped
- A pinch of sea salt
- ½ teaspoon ground cinnamon
- ½ teaspoon vanilla extract

1. Place the bread in a lightly greased baking dish.
2. In a mixing bowl, thoroughly combine the remaining ingredients.
3. Pour the milk mixture over the bread cubes. Set aside for 15 minutes to soak.
4. Place the baking dish in the air fryer basket or wire rack. and bake in the preheated instant pot at 180°C for about 20 minutes or until the custard is set but still a little wobbly.
5. Serve at room temperature. Bon appétit!

Cheesy Macaroni
Prep time: 5 minutes | Cook time: 15 minutes | Serves 4

- 2 cups macaroni
- 1 cup milk
- 2 cups grated Mozzarella cheese
- ½ teaspoon Italian seasoning
- Sea salt and ground black pepper, to taste
- ½ teaspoon garlic powder
- 1 teaspoon dry mustard

1. Cook the macaroni according to the package directions.
2. Drain the macaroni and place them in a lightly greased baking dish.
3. Fold in the remaining ingredients and stir to combine.
4. Place the baking dish in the air fryer basket or wire rack. and bake in the preheated instant pot at 180°C for 15 minutes.
5. Serve garnished with fresh Italian herbs, if desired.
6. Bon appétit!

Air Fried Butter Toast
Prep time: 5 minutes | Cook time: 8 minutes | Serves 3

- 2 eggs
- ½ cup milk
- 2 tablespoons butter, room temperature
- 1 teaspoon vanilla extract
- ¼ teaspoon grated nutmeg
- ½ teaspoon cinnamon powder
- 3 slices challah bread

1. In a mixing bowl, thoroughly combine the eggs, milk, butter, vanilla, nutmeg, and cinnamon.
2. Then dip each piece of bread into the egg mixture; place the bread slices in a lightly greased air fryer basket or wire rack.
3. and air fry in the preheated instant pot at 170°C for 8 minutes. Flip the bread slices halfway through.
4. Enjoy!

Chocolate Chips muesli
Prep time: 10 minutes | Cook time: 15 minutes | Serves 8

- ½ cup old-fashioned oats
- ¼ cup unsweetened coconut flakes
- ¼ cup quinoa flakes
- ¼ cup slivered almonds
- ¼ cup chopped hazelnuts
- ¼ cup chia seeds
- 1 teaspoon ground cinnamon
- A pinch of grated nutmeg
- A pinch of sea salt
- 2 tablespoons coconut oil
- ¼ cup maple syrup
- 1 teaspoon vanilla extract
- ½ cup chocolate chips

1. Thoroughly combine all ingredients in a lightly greased baking dish.
2. Place the baking dish in the air fryer basket or wire rack. and bake in the preheated instant pot at 180°C for 15 minutes, stirring every 5 minutes.
3. Store at room temperature in an airtight container for up to three weeks.
4. Bon appétit!

Rice with Scallions
Prep time: 5 minutes | Cook time: 10 minutes | Serves 4

- 2 cups jasmine rice, cooked
- 1 cup vegetable broth
- 1 teaspoon garlic powder
- ½ cup chopped scallions
- 2 tablespoons butter, room temperature
- flake salt and red pepper, to taste

1. Thoroughly combine all ingredients in a lightly greased baking dish.
2. Place the baking dish in the air fryer basket or wire rack. and bake in the preheated instant pot at 180°C for 10 minutes or until cooked through.
3. Bon appétit!

Carrot and Green Peas Rice
Prep time: 5 minutes | Cook time: 10 minutes | Serves 4

- 2 cups multigrain rice, cooked
- 1 small onion, finely chopped
- 1 teaspoon minced garlic
- 2 tablespoons sesame oil
- 1 egg, whisked
- 2 tablespoons soy sauce
- 1 carrot, chopped
- 1 cup green peas
- Sea salt and red chili flakes, to taste

1. Thoroughly combine all ingredients in a lightly greased baking dish.
2. Place the baking dish in the air fryer basket or wire rack. and bake in the preheated instant pot at 180°C for 10 minutes or until cooked through.
3. Bon appétit!

Pumpkin Porridge with Chocolate
Prep time: 5 minutes | Cook time: 12 minutes | Serves 5

- ½ cup old-fashioned oats
- ½ cup quinoa flakes
- ¼ cup chopped pecans
- 2 tablespoons ground chia seeds
- 2 tablespoons ground flax seeds
- 1 teaspoon vanilla essence
- 2 ounces (57 g) dark chocolate chips
- ½ cup tinned pumpkin
- ½ cup almond milk

1. Thoroughly combine all ingredients in a mixing bowl. Spoon the mixture into a lightly greased baking dish.
2. Place the baking dish in the air fryer basket or wire rack. and bake in the preheated instant pot at 190°C for 12 minutes.
3. Serve immediately. Bon appétit!

Chawal ke Pakore with Cheese
Prep time: 5 minutes | Cook time: 15 minutes | Serves 4

- 1 cup rice flour
- ½ onion, chopped
- 2 garlic cloves, minced
- 2 tablespoons butter, room temperature
- 1 teaspoon paprika
- 1 teaspoon cumin powder
- ½ cup crumbled Paneer cheese

1. Mix all ingredients until everything is well combined. Form the mixture into patties. Transfer to the air fryer basket or wire rack.
2. and air fry in the preheated instant pot at 190°C for 15 minutes. Flip the patties halfway through.
3. Bon appétit!

Rice Cheese Casserole
Prep time: 10 minutes | Cook time: 10 minutes | Serves 4

- 1 small shallot, minced
- 2 garlic cloves, minced
- 2 tablespoons olive oil
- ½ teaspoon paprika
- 2 eggs, whisked
- 1 cup half-and-half
- 1 cup shredded Cheddar cheese
- 2 cups cooked brown rice
- 1 tablespoon chopped Italian parsley leaves
- 1 cup cream of celery soup
- Sea salt and freshly ground black pepper, to taste

1. Thoroughly combine all ingredients in a lightly greased baking dish.
2. Place the baking dish in the air fryer basket or wire rack. and bake in the preheated instant pot at 180°C for 10 minutes or until cooked through.
3. Bon appétit!

Millet Porridge with Sultanas
Prep time: 5 minutes | Cook time: 12 minutes | Serves 5

- ½ cup old-fashioned oats
- ½ cup millet, rinsed and drained
- 2 tablespoons ground flax seeds
- ½ cup Sultanas
- 2 cups coconut milk
- 2 tablespoons coconut oil
- A pinch of salt
- A pinch of ground cloves

1. Thoroughly combine all ingredients in a mixing bowl. Spoon the mixture into a lightly greased baking dish.
2. Place the baking dish in the air fryer basket or wire rack. and bake in the preheated instant pot at 190°C for 12 minutes.
3. Serve immediately. Bon appétit!

Creamy Cornbread Casserole
Prep time: 5 minutes | Cook time: 12 minutes | Serves 6

- 3 eggs
- 2 tablespoons coconut oil, room temperature
- ½ cup double cream
- 1 teaspoon vanilla
- ½ cup Demerara sugar
- ½ teaspoon ground cinnamon
- A pinch of grated nutmeg
- A pinch of salt
- 6 slices sweet corn bread

1. In a mixing bowl, thoroughly combine the eggs, coconut oil, double cream, vanilla, sugar, cinnamon, nutmeg, and salt.
2. Then, place the cornbread slices in a lightly greased baking dish. Pour the custard mixture over the cornbread slices.
3. Place the baking dish in the air fryer basket or wire rack. and bake in the preheated instant pot at 170°C for 12 minutes.
4. Enjoy!

Cheesy Carbonara with Pancetta
Prep time: 10 minutes | Cook time: 10 minutes | Serves 4

- 2 cups Arborio rice, cooked
- 2 tablespoons sesame oil
- 1 shallot, chopped
- ½ cup white Italian wine
- ½ cup double cream
- Coarse sea salt and freshly ground black pepper, to taste
- 4 tablespoons chopped pancetta
- 1 cup grated Parmesan cheese
- 1 tablespoon chopped fresh Italian parsley

1. Thoroughly combine all ingredients in a lightly greased baking dish.
2. Place the baking dish in the air fryer basket or wire rack. and bake in the preheated instant pot at 180°C for 10 minutes or until cooked through.
3. Bon appétit!

Chapter 8
Side Dishes

Turmeric Cauliflower Rice
Prep time: 5 minutes | Cook time: 20 minutes | Serves 4

- 1 big cauliflower, florets separated and riced
- 1 and ½ cups chicken stock
- 1 tablespoon olive oil
- Salt and black pepper to the taste
- ½ teaspoon turmeric powder

1. In a pan that fits the air fryer, combine the cauliflower with the oil and the rest of the ingredients, toss, introduce in the air fryer and cook at 180°C for 20 minutes.
2. Divide between plates and serve as a side dish.

Mushroom Cakes
Prep time: 10 minutes | Cook time: 8 minutes | Serves 4

- 9 oz mushrooms, finely chopped
- ¼ cup coconut flour
- 1 teaspoon salt
- 1 egg, beaten
- 3 oz Cheddar cheese, shredded
- 1 teaspoon dried parsley
- ½ teaspoon ground black pepper
- 1 teaspoon sesame oil
- 1 oz spring onion, chopped

1. In the mixing bowl mix up chopped mushrooms, coconut flour, salt, egg, dried parsley, ground black pepper, and minced onion. Stir the mixture until smooth and add Cheddar cheese.
2. Stir it with the help of the fork, Preheat the air fryer to 190°C. Line the air fryer pan with baking paper. With the help of the spoon make the medium size patties and put them in the pan.
3. Sprinkle the patties with sesame oil and cook for 4 minutes from each side.

Cauliflower and Tomato Bake
Prep time: 5 minutes | Cook time: 20 minutes | Serves 2

- 1 cup heavy whipping cream
- 2 tablespoons basil pesto
- Salt and black pepper to the taste
- Juice of ½ lemon
- 1 pound cauliflower, florets separated
- 4 ounces cherry tomatoes, halved
- 3 tablespoons ghee, melted
- 7 ounces cheddar cheese, grated

1. Grease a baking pan that fits the air fryer with the ghee. Add the cauliflower, lemon juice, salt, pepper, the pesto and the cream and toss gently.
2. Add the tomatoes, sprinkle the cheese on top, introduce the pan in the fryer and cook at 190°C for 20 minutes. Divide between plates and serve as a side dish.

Turmeric Tofu
Prep time: 10 minutes | Cook time: 9 minutes | Serves 2

- 6 oz tofu, cubed
- 1 teaspoon avocado oil
- 1 teaspoon apple cider vinegar
- 1 garlic clove, diced
- ¼ teaspoon ground turmeric
- ¼ teaspoon ground paprika
- ½ teaspoon dried Coriander
- ¼ teaspoon lemon zest, grated

1. In the bowl mix up avocado oil, apple cider vinegar, diced garlic, ground turmeric, paprika, Coriander, and lime zest.
2. Coat the tofu cubes in the oil mixture. Preheat the air fryer to 200°C. Put the tofu cubes in the air fryer and cook them for 9 minutes.
3. Shake the tofu cubes from time to time during cooking.

Coconut Chives Sprouts

Prep time: 5 minutes | Cook time: 20 minutes | Serves 4

- 1 pound Brussels sprouts, trimmed and halved
- Salt and black pepper to the taste
- 2 tablespoons ghee, melted
- ½ cup coconut cream
- 2 tablespoons garlic, minced
- 1 tablespoon chives, chopped

1. In your air fryer, mix the sprouts with the rest of the ingredients except the chives, toss well, introduce in the air fryer and cook them at 190°C for 20 minutes.
2. Divide the Brussels sprouts between plates, sprinkle the chives on top and serve as a side dish.

Cheesy courgette Tots

Prep time: 15 minutes | Cook time: 6 minutes | Serves 4

- 1 courgette, grated
- ½ cup Mozzarella, shredded
- 1 egg, beaten
- 2 tablespoons almond flour
- ½ teaspoon ground black pepper
- 1 teaspoon coconut oil, melted

1. Mix up grated courgette, shredded Mozzarella, egg, almond flour, and ground black pepper. Then make the small courgette tots with the help of the fingertips. Preheat the air fryer to 190°C.
2. Place the courgette tots in the air fryer basket or wire rack and cook for 3 minutes from each side or until the courgette tots are golden brown.

Creamy Broccoli and Cauliflower
Prep time: 5 minutes | Cook time: 20 minutes | Serves 4

- 15 ounces broccoli florets
- 10 ounces cauliflower florets
- 1 leek, chopped
- 2 spring onions, chopped
- Salt and black pepper to the taste
- 2 ounces butter, melted
- 2 tablespoons mustard
- 1 cup Soured cream
- 5 ounces mozzarella cheese, shredded

1. In a baking pan that fits the air fryer, add the butter and spread it well. Add the broccoli, cauliflower and the rest of the ingredients except the mozzarella and toss.
2. Sprinkle the cheese on top, introduce the pan in the air fryer and cook at 190°C for 20 minutes. Divide between plates and serve as a side dish.

Mushroom Tots
Prep time: 15 minutes | Cook time: 6 minutes | Serves 2

- 1 cup white mushrooms, grinded
- 1 teaspoon onion powder
- 1 egg yolk
- 3 teaspoons flax meal
- ½ teaspoon ground black pepper
- 1 teaspoon avocado oil
- 1 tablespoon coconut flour

1. Mix up grinded white mushrooms with onion powder, egg yolk, flax meal, ground black pepper, and coconut flour. When the mixture is smooth and homogenous, make the mushroom tots.
2. Preheat the air fryer to 200°C. Sprinkle the air fryer basket or wire rack with melted coconut oil and put the mushroom tots inside. Cook them for 3 minutes.
3. Then flip the mushroom tots on another side and cook them for 2-3 minutes more or until they are light brown.

Mozzarella Risotto
Prep time: 5 minutes | Cook time: 20 minutes | Serves 4

- 1 pound white mushrooms, sliced
- ¼ cup mozzarella, shredded
- 1 cauliflower head, florets separated and riced
- 1 cup chicken stock
- 1 tablespoon thyme, chopped
- 1 teaspoon Italian seasoning
- A pinch of salt and black pepper
- 2 tablespoons olive oil

1. Heat up a pan that fits the air fryer with the oil over medium heat, add the cauliflower rice and the mushrooms, toss and cook for a couple of minutes. Add the rest of the ingredients except the thyme, toss, put the pan in the air fryer and cook at 180°C for 20 minutes.
2. Divide the risotto between plates and serve with thyme sprinkled on top.

Creamy Cauliflower Tots
Prep time: 15 minutes | Cook time: 8 minutes | Serves 4

- 1 teaspoon cream cheese
- 5 oz Parmesan Cheese, shredded
- 1 cup cauliflower, chopped, boiled
- ¼ teaspoon garlic powder
- 1 teaspoon sunflower oil

1. Put the boiled cauliflower in the blender. Add garlic powder, cream cheese, and shredded Parmesan Cheese.
2. Blend the mixture until smooth. Make the cauliflower tots and refrigerate them for 10 minutes. Meanwhile, preheat the air fryer to 180°C.
3. Place the cauliflower inside the air fryer basket or wire rack and sprinkle with sunflower oil. Cook the tots for 4 minutes from each side.

Spinach Salad
Prep time: 5 minutes | Cook time: 10 minutes | Serves 4

- 1 pound baby spinach
- Salt and black pepper to the taste
- 1 tablespoon mustard
- Cooking spray
- ¼ cup apple cider vinegar
- 1 tablespoon chives, chopped

1. Grease a pan that fits your air fryer with Cooking spray , combine all the ingredients, introduce the pan in the fryer and cook at 350 degrees F for 10 minutes.
2. Divide between plates and serve as a side dish.

Chapter 9
Starters and Snacks

Avocado Chips
Prep time: 15 minutes | Cook time: 10 minutes | Serves 4

- 1 egg
- 1 tablespoon lime juice
- ⅛ teaspoon chili sauce
- 2 tablespoons flour
- ¾ cup panko bread crumbs
- ¼ cup cornmeal
- ¼ teaspoon salt
- 1 large avocado, pitted, peeled, and cut into ½-inch slices
- Cooking spray

1. Whisk together the egg, lime juice, and chili sauce in a small bowl.
2. On a sheet of wax paper, place the flour. In a separate sheet of wax paper, combine the bread crumbs, cornmeal, and salt.
3. Dredge the avocado slices one at a time in the flour, then in the egg mixture, finally roll them in the bread crumb mixture to coat well.
4. Place the breaded avocado slices in the air flow racks and mist them with cooking spray.
5. Slide the racks into the air fryer. Press the Power Button. Cook at 200°C for 10 minutes.
6. When cooking is complete, the slices should be nicely browned and crispy. Transfer the avocado slices to a plate and serve.

Baked Sardines with Tomato Sauce
Prep time: 10 minutes | Cook time: 20 minutes | Serves 4

- 2 pounds (907 g) fresh Sardines
- 3 tablespoons olive oil, divided
- 4 Roma tomatoes, peeled and chopped
- 1 small onion, sliced thinly
- Zest of 1 orange
- Sea salt and freshly ground pepper, to taste
- 2 tablespoons whole-wheat bread crumbs
- ½ cup white wine

1. Brush a sheet pan with a little olive oil. Set aside.
2. Rinse the Sardines under running water. Slit the belly, remove the spine and butterfly the fish. Set aside.
3. Heat the remaining olive oil in a large frying pan. Add the tomatoes, onion, orange zest, salt and pepper to the frying pan and simmer for 20 minutes, or until the mixture thickens and softens.
4. Place half the sauce in the bottom of the sheet pan. Arrange the Sardines on top and spread the remaining half the sauce over the fish. Sprinkle with the bread crumbs and drizzle with the white wine.
5. Slide the pan into the air fryer. Press the Power Button. Cook at 200°C for 20 minutes.
6. When cooking is complete, remove from the air fryer. Serve immediately.

Broiled Prosciutto-Wrapped Pears
Prep time: 12 minutes | Cook time: 6 minutes | Serves 8

- 2 large, ripe Anjou pears
- 4 thin slices Parma prosciutto
- 2 teaspoons aged balsamic vinegar

1. Peel the pears. Slice into 8 wedges and cut out the core from each wedge.
2. Cut the prosciutto into 8 long strips. Wrap each pear wedge with a strip of prosciutto. Place the wrapped pears in a sheet pan.
3. Slide the pan into the air fryer. Cook for 6 minutes.
4. After 2 or 3 minutes, check the pears. The pears should be turned over if the prosciutto is beginning to crisp up and brown. Return to the air fryer and continue cooking.
5. When cooking is complete, remove from the air fryer. Drizzle the pears with the balsamic vinegar and serve warm.

Bruschetta with Tomato and Basil
Prep time: 5 minutes | Cook time: 3 minutes | Serves 6

- 4 tomatoes, diced
- ⅓ cup shredded fresh basil
- ¼ cup shredded Parmesan cheese
- 1 tablespoon balsamic vinegar
- 1 tablespoon minced garlic
- 1 teaspoon olive oil
- 1 teaspoon salt
- 1 teaspoon freshly ground black pepper
- 1 loaf French bread, cut into 1-inch-thick slices
- Cooking spray

1. Mix the tomatoes and basil in a medium bowl. Add the cheese, vinegar, garlic, olive oil, salt, and pepper and stir until well incorporated. Set aside.
2. Spritz the air flow racks with cooking spray and lay the bread slices in the racks. Spray the slices with cooking spray.
3. Slide the racks into the air fryer. Press the Power Button. Cook at 120°C for 3 minutes.
4. When cooking is complete, remove from the air fryer to a plate. Top each slice with a generous spoonful of the tomato mixture and serve.

Browned Ricotta with Capers and Lemon

Prep time: 10 minutes | Cook time: 8 minutes | Serves 4 to 6

- 1½ cups whole milk ricotta cheese
- 2 tablespoons extra-virgin olive oil
- 2 tablespoons capers, rinsed
- Zest of 1 lemon, plus more for garnish
- 1 teaspoon finely chopped fresh rosemary
- Pinch crushed red pepper flakes
- Salt and freshly ground black pepper, to taste
- 1 tablespoon grated Parmesan cheese

1. In a mixing bowl, stir together the ricotta cheese, olive oil, capers, lemon zest, rosemary, red pepper flakes, salt, and pepper until well combined.
2. Spread the mixture evenly in a baking dish.
3. Slide the baking dish into the air fryer. Press the Power Button. Cook at 190°C for 8 minutes.
4. When cooking is complete, the top should be nicely browned. Remove from the air fryer and top with a sprinkle of grated Parmesan cheese. Garnish with the lemon zest and serve warm.

Prawn Toasts with Sesame Seeds

Prep time: 15 minutes | Cook time: 8 minutes | Serves 4 to 6

- ½ pound (227 g) raw Prawn, peeled and deveined
- 1 egg, beaten
- 2 scallions, chopped, plus more for garnish
- 2 tablespoons chopped fresh Coriander
- 2 teaspoons grated fresh ginger
- 1 to 2 teaspoons sriracha sauce
- 1 teaspoon soy sauce
- ½ teaspoon toasted sesame oil
- 6 slices thinly sliced white sandwich bread
- ½ cup sesame seeds
- Cooking spray
- Thai chili sauce, for serving

1. In a food processor, add the Prawn, egg, scallions, Coriander, ginger, sriracha sauce, soy sauce and sesame oil, and pulse until chopped finely. Stop the food processor occasionally to scrape down the sides. Transfer the Prawn mixture to a bowl.
2. On a clean work surface, cut the crusts off the sandwich bread. Using a brush, generously brush one side of each slice of bread with Prawn mixture.
3. Place the sesame seeds on a plate. Press bread slices, Prawn-side down, into sesame seeds to coat evenly. Cut each slice diagonally into quarters.
4. Spritz the air flow racks with cooking spray. Spread the coated slices in a single layer in the air flow racks.
5. Slide the racks into the air fryer. Press the Power Button. Cook at 200°C for 8 minutes.
6. Flip the bread slices halfway through.
7. When cooking is complete, they should be golden and crispy. Remove from the air fryer to a plate and let cool for 5 minutes. Top with the chopped scallions and serve warm with Thai chili sauce.

Tuna Melts with Scallions

Prep time: 10 minutes | **Cook time:** 6 minutes | **Serves 6**

- 2 (5- to 6-ounce / 142- to 170-g) cans oil-packed tuna, drained
- 1 large scallion, chopped
- 1 small stalk celery, chopped
- ⅓ cup mayonnaise
- 1 tablespoon chopped fresh dill
- 1 tablespoon capers, drained
- ¼ teaspoon celery salt
- 12 slices cocktail rye bread
- 2 tablespoons butter, melted
- 6 slices sharp Cheddar cheese

1. In a medium bowl, stir together the tuna, scallion, celery, mayonnaise, dill, capers and celery salt.
2. Brush one side of the bread slices with the butter. Arrange the bread slices on a sheet pan, buttered-side down. Scoop a heaping tablespoon of the tuna mixture on each slice of bread, spreading it out even to the edges.
3. Cut the cheese slices to fit the dimensions of the bread and place a cheese slice on each piece.
4. Slide the pan into the air fryer. Press the Power Button. Cook at 190°C for 6 minutes.
5. After 4 minutes, remove from the air fryer and check the tuna melts. The tuna melts are done when the cheese has melted and the tuna is heated through. If needed, continue cooking.
6. When cooking is complete, remove from the air fryer. Use a spatula to transfer the tuna melts to a clean work surface and slice each one in half diagonally. Serve warm.

Turkey Bacon-Wrapped Dates

Prep time: 10 minutes | **Cook time:** 6 minutes | **Makes 16 Starters**

- 16 whole dates, pitted
- 16 whole almonds
- 6 to 8 strips turkey bacon, cut in half

SPECIAL EQUIPMENT:
- 16 Cocktail Sticks, soaked in water for at least 30 minutes

1. On a flat work surface, stuff each pitted date with a whole almond.
2. Wrap half slice of bacon around each date and secure it with a toothpick.
3. Place the bacon-wrapped dates in the air flow racks.
4. Slide the racks into the air fryer. Press the Power Button. Cook at 200°C for 6 minutes.
5. When cooking is complete, transfer the dates to a paper towel-lined plate to drain. Serve hot.

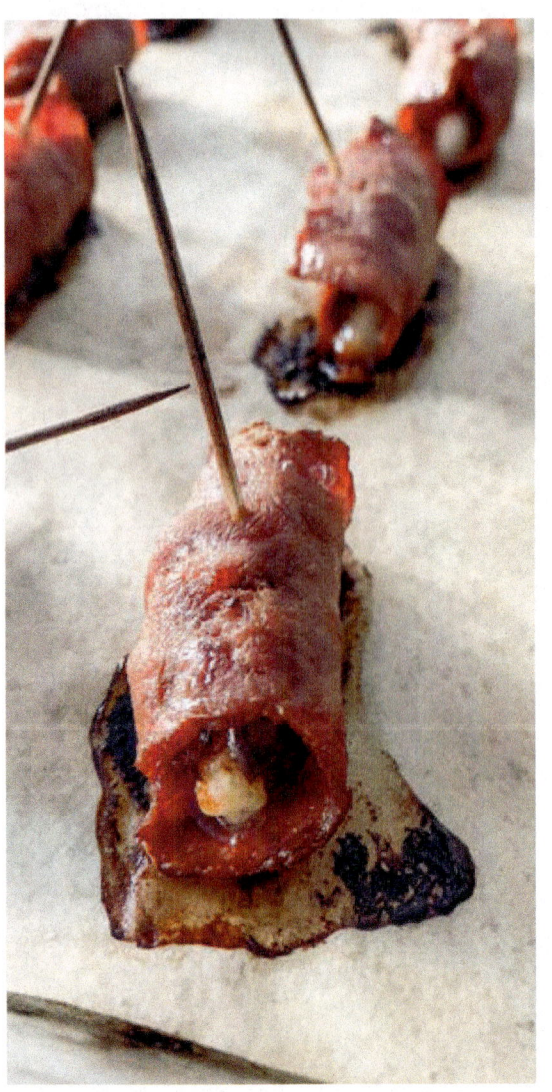

Appendix 1 Measurement Conversion Chart

Volume Equivalents (Dry)	
US STANDARD	**METRIC (APPROXIMATE)**
1/8 teaspoon	0.5 mL
1/4 teaspoon	1 mL
1/2 teaspoon	2 mL
3/4 teaspoon	4 mL
1 teaspoon	5 mL
1 tablespoon	15 mL
1/4 cup	59 mL
1/2 cup	118 mL
3/4 cup	177 mL
1 cup	235 mL
2 cups	475 mL
3 cups	700 mL
4 cups	1 L

Volume Equivalents (Liquid)		
US STANDARD	**US STANDARD (OUNCES)**	**METRIC (APPROXIMATE)**
2 tablespoons	1 fl.oz.	30 mL
1/4 cup	2 fl.oz.	60 mL
1/2 cup	4 fl.oz.	120 mL
1 cup	8 fl.oz.	240 mL
1 1/2 cup	12 fl.oz.	355 mL
2 cups or 1 pint	16 fl.oz.	475 mL
4 cups or 1 quart	32 fl.oz.	1 L
1 gallon	128 fl.oz.	4 L

Weight Equivalents	
US STANDARD	**METRIC (APPROXIMATE)**
1 ounce	28 g
2 ounces	57 g
5 ounces	142 g
10 ounces	284 g
15 ounces	425 g
16 ounces (1 pound)	455 g
1.5 pounds	680 g
2 pounds	907 g

Temperatures Equivalents	
FAHRENHEIT(F)	**CELSIUS(C) APPROXIMATE)**
225 °F	107 °C
250 °F	120 ° °C
275 °F	135 °C
300 °F	150 °C
325 °F	160 °C
350 °F	180 °C
375 °F	190 °C
400 °F	205 °C
425 °F	220 °C
450 °F	235 °C
475 °F	245 °C
500 °F	260 °C

Appendix 2 The Dirty Dozen and Clean Fifteen

The Environmental Working Group (EWG) is a nonprofit, nonpartisan organization dedicated to protecting human health and the environment Its mission is to empower people to live healthier lives in a healthier environment. This organization publishes an annual list of the twelve kinds of produce, in sequence, that have the highest amount of pesticide residue-the Dirty Dozen-as well as a list of the fifteen kinds of produce that have the least amount of pesticide residue-the Clean Fifteen.

THE DIRTY DOZEN	
The 2016 Dirty Dozen includes the following produce. These are considered among the year's most important produce to buy organic:	
Strawberries	Spinach
Apples	Tomatoes
Nectarines	Bell peppers
Peaches	Cherry tomatoes
Celery	Cucumbers
Grapes	Kale/collard greens
Cherries	Hot peppers
The Dirty Dozen list contains two additional items kale/collard greens and hot peppers-because they tend to contain trace levels of highly hazardous pesticides.	

THE CLEAN FIFTEEN	
The least critical to buy organically are the Clean Fifteen list. The following are on the 2016 list:	
Avocados	Papayas
Corn	Kiw
Pineapples	Eggplant
Cabbage	Honeydew
Sweet peas	Grapefruit
Onions	Cantaloupe
Asparagus	Cauliflower
Mangos	
Some of the sweet corn sold in the United States are made from genetically engineered (GE) seedstock. Buy organic varieties of these crops to avoid GE produce.	

Appendix 3 Index

A

agave syrup 46, 49
all-purpose flour 46
almond 50, 52, 53
almond flour 22, 59
almond milk 53
apple 46
apple cider vinegar 21, 23, 58, 61
asparagus 26
avocado 21, 22, 24, 25, 27, 28, 58
]avocado oil 21, 22, 24, 25, 27, 58, 60

B

baking powder 46, 48
basmati rice 47
bread 49, 50, 51, 55
bread crumbs 48
Brioche bread 50
broccoli 48, 60
brown rice 54
brown sugar 46, 50, 55
Brussels sprout 59
butter 27, 48, 51, 52, 54, 60

C

carrot 53
cauliflower 27, 57, 58, 60, 61
cayenne pepper 47
challah bread 51
Cheddar cheese 54, 57
chia seeds 52, 53
chicken 21, 22, 23, 24, 25, 26, 27, 28, 61
chicken breasts 25, 28
chicken drumsticks 25
chicken stock 57
chicken thighs 27
chicken wings 23, 24, 26
chili flakes 53
chili powder 27
chives 59, 61
chocolate chips 52
chopped almonds 50
chopped hazelnuts 52
cilantro 58
cinnamon 25, 49, 50, 51, 52, 55
cinnamon powder 46, 50, 51
coarse salt 46
cocoa powder 46
coconut 21, 23, 24, 25, 26, 27, 28, 46, 49, 50, 52, 55, 57, 60
coconut cream 27, 59
coconut extract 46
coconut flour 27, 28, 46, 57, 60
coconut milk 49, 55
coconut oil 21, 23, 24, 26, 46, 49, 50, 52, 55, 59, 60
coconut shred 25
coriander 23
corn 55
Cornish hens 21
corn kernels 48
cream cheese 61
cream of celery soup 54
cumin powder 54
curry leaves 47

D

dark chocolate 53
dark chocolate chips 53
dried basil 24
dried cherries 49
dried cilantro 58
dried cranberries 49
dried figs 50
dried parsley 57
dry mustard 51

E

egg 25, 27, 28, 46, 48, 49, 50, 51, 53, 54, 55, 57, 59, 60
eggnog 50
Erythritol 24

F

fig 50
flax meal 60
flax seeds 53, 55
fresh cilantro 47
fresh Italian herbs 48, 51
fresh parsley 47

G

Gai yang spices 21
garlic 23, 27, 47, 48, 53, 54, 58, 59, 61
garlic powder 23, 47, 51, 52, 61
ghee 58, 59
ginger 25
green beans 28
ground cloves 49, 55

H

half-and-half 54
hazelnut 52
hazelnuts 28
heavy cream 48, 55
heavy whipping cream 58
honey 49

I

instant coffee granules	46
Italian parsley leaves	54
Italian seasoning	51, 61

J

jasmine rice	52

K

keto BBQ sauce	26
kosher salt	49

L

lemon	22, 58
lemon juice	22, 58
lemon zest	22, 58
lime zest	58

M

macaroni	51
maple syrup	52
milk	46, 49, 50, 51
millet	55
Monterey Jack cheese	61
mozzarella	60, 61
mozzarella cheese	60
multigrain rice	47, 53
mushroom	57, 60, 61
mustard	60, 61

N

nutmeg	27, 46, 51, 52, 55

O

old-fashioned oats	52, 53, 55
olive oil	25, 26, 27, 28, 47, 54, 57, 61
onion	25, 26, 47, 48, 53, 54, 57, 60
onion powder	25, 26, 60
oregano	27, 28

P

pancetta	55
Paneer cheese	54
paprika	21, 26, 54, 58
Parmesan cheese	48, 55
parsley	27, 28, 55
peas	53
pecan	53
pesto	58
pork	25
pork rinds	25
Provolone	27
Provolone cheese	27
prune	49
pumpkin	53

Q

quinoa	48
quinoa flakes	52, 53

R

rice	47, 54, 55
rice flour	54
rolled oats	46

S

scallion	47, 52
self-rising flour	46
sesame oil	53, 55, 57
shallot	54, 55
slivered almonds	52
sour cream	60
soy sauce	53
spinach	61
sugar	55
Sultanas	55
sunflower oil	61
sweet corn bread	55
sweet raisin bread	49

T

taco seasoning	24
thyme	27, 61
tofu	58
tomato	58
turmeric	58
turmeric powder	57

U

unsweetened coconut flakes	52

V

vanilla	46, 49, 50, 51, 52, 53, 55
vanilla essence	53
vanilla extract	46, 49, 50, 51, 52
vegetable broth	47, 52

W

whole-wheat flour	48

Z

zucchini	59

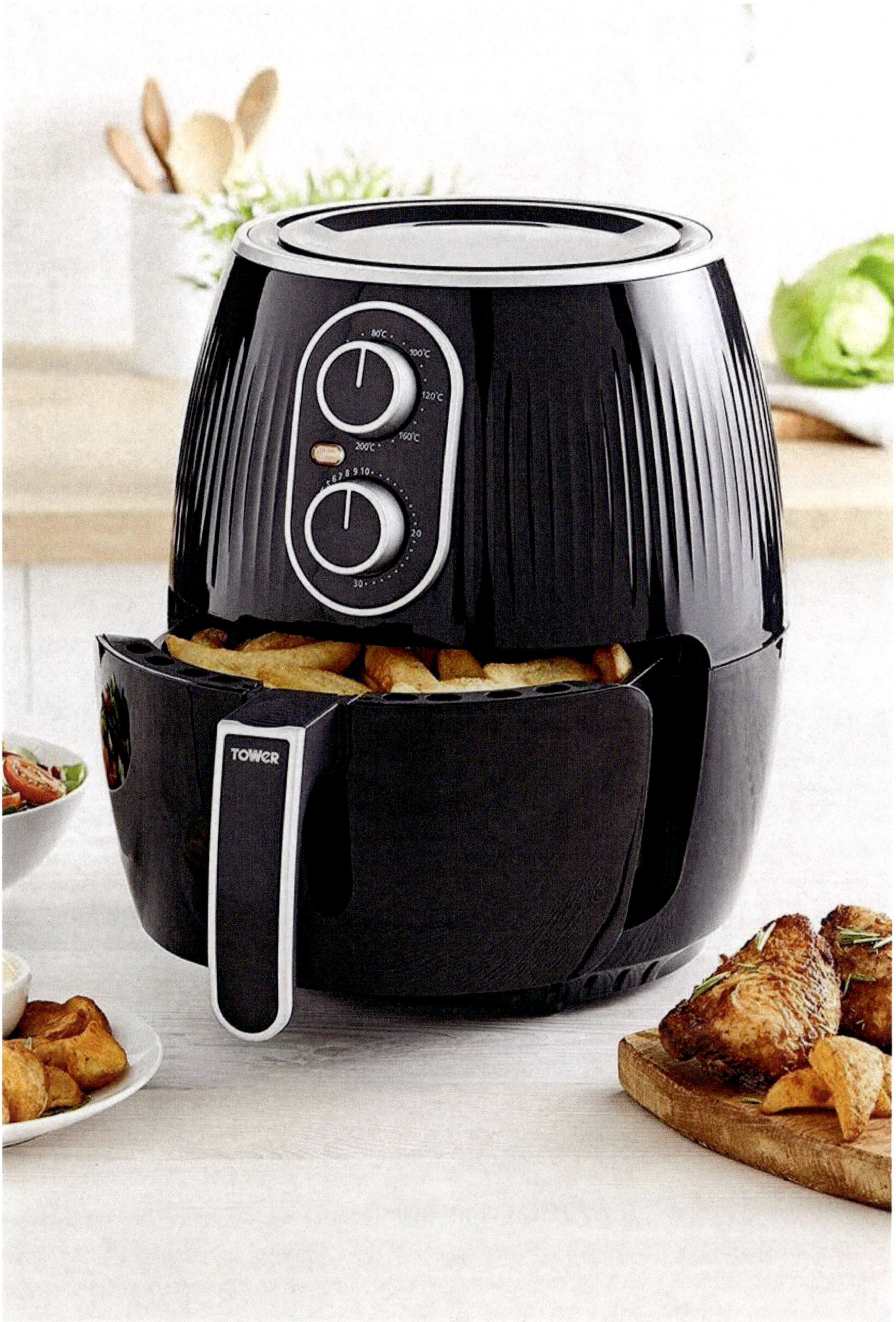
80°C
100°C
120°C
160°C
200°C
20
30
TOWER

CATHERINE C. KIMBREL

Printed in Great Britain
by Amazon